HOW TO PROTECT
MY MILLION

STRATEGIES TO IDENTIFY
AND
AVOID SWINDLERS

Joan,
All the best!
Ward

Ward Garner

HOW TO PROTECT MY MILLION
STRATEGIES TO IDENTIFY AND AVOID SWINDLERS

Certified Financial Planner Board of Standards Inc. owns the certification marks CFP®, CERTIFIED FINANCIAL PLANNER™, CFP® (with plaque design) and CFP® (with flame design) in the U.S., which it awards to individuals who successfully complete CFP Board's initial and ongoing certification requirements.

To contact the author, Ward Garner, visit:

Website .... : HowToProtectMyMillion.com

Email .... : HowToProtectMyMillion@gmail.com

LinkedIn .... : www.linkedin.com/in/wardgarner

Facebook .... : www.facebook.com/HowToProtectMyMillion/

Printed in the United States of America

— Finance, Personal

To contact the publisher, inCredible Messages Press, visit
www.inCredibleMessages.com

ISBN 978-0-9908265-8-3 paperback

ISBN 978-0-9908265-9-0 eBook

Book coach .... : Bonnie Budzowski

Cover design .... : Bobbie Fox Fratangelo

Author photograph ... : Mary Beth Kratsas, MBK Photography

DEDICATION

To my wife, Lori, and to the clients who have trusted me over the years as their financial advisor and friend.

Acknowledgements

NONE OF US SUCCEEDS IN LIFE WITHOUT THE HELP of hundreds of others. I gratefully acknowledge my parents, Walter and Dorothy Garner. The youngest of their six children, my parents understood what I needed to grow. They loved me, taught me values, and encouraged me to learn discipline. I first found that discipline in the U.S. Airforce, and then applied it by getting a college education, then my CERTIFIED FINANCIAL PLANNER™ (CFP®) designation, and then serving my clients with integrity in the financial industry.

I thank my lovely wife, Lori, for her undying loyalty and dedication. Lori is everything I could hope for in a wife. Without Lori's blessings and hard work on our home front, accomplishments such as this book would not be possible.

My friend and business associate, Ken Como, has been with me for my entire career in financial services. I'm grateful for everything our friendship has meant to me over the years. Ken's dedication to clients has always been an inspiration to me.

Another friend and business associate, Joseph DeAndrea, was instrumental in keeping me on the career path of professional financial planning and investment management. In the early 1990's when I lived and died by the commissions earned as commissioned broker, I would have chosen another career path without Joe's encouragement and support. Thank you.

Bill Few was a mentor extraordinaire. He taught me, among other things, to protect my clients from themselves as well as from others.

I could not have completed this book without the help of my coach, editor, and publication guide, Bonnie Budzowski. I knew when I met Bonnie that I could count on her competence and commitment to high quality, and I was not disappointed. Her guidance was always timely and helpful.

I'm grateful to Robert Williams, who was my Rotary International sponsor. I like Rotary because it's like capitalism; it's very efficient. Rotary International is the greatest humanitarian organization in the world and the only organization of its kind in the United Nations.

CONTENTS

INTRODUCTION

MY STORY:
HOW I UNWITTINGLY BECAME A FIDUCIARY

THE YEAR WAS 1989, a time when good employment opportunities were scarce, especially in a small town like St. Mary's, Pennsylvania, 100 miles from the nearest city. At age 28, an Air Force veteran and fresh college graduate, I consulted my second cousin, an unemployment counselor.

He said, "Ward, you're a big fish in a small pond. You need to move to the city. Your cousin Rupert lives in Pittsburgh. As a stockbroker, he makes tons of money and drives fancy cars. You would make a fine stockbroker. It's just sales."

My first mistake was accepting this as good advice. Before long, I was on the path to becoming a professional swindler. Here's how it happened.

It began with a healthy urge to succeed and have the good life. After my five-year commitment to the U. S. Air Force, I enrolled at the University of Pittsburgh at Bradford, majoring in Business Management and minoring in Economics. I supplemented my savings from the Air Force by starting Sounds Great Disc Jockey Entertainment Service. The proceeds from savings and disc jockey gigs carried me through college and beyond.

Accepting my second cousin's advice, I moved to Pittsburgh, buoyed by hopes of money and fancy cars. My younger cousin, Rupert, the one with money and cars, explained that the stockbroker job he had to offer was not a salaried position, nor did it offer a paid training program. This was a commission-only job, but it came with the title of stockbroker. I liked the title and the potential of a high income in the future. Looking back, the whole thing seemed too good to be true—and it was.

Before earning stockbroker commissions, I had to be licensed. Moreover, I had to pay for study materials and to take the test that would result in the appropriate licensing. Thankfully, disc jockey gigs paid the bills through this period. I was roaring to go, and having no responsibilities other than myself, I completed the licensing process in six months. In March of 1990, with a license to sell securities, I was ready to start working.

My first clue that something was wrong came when I was prohibited from selling to my natural market, i.e., friends and family. The owners of the group had encouraged me to get my license, but they hadn't given me the whole picture. I was so eager to earn that I hadn't asked good questions—just trusted. After all, Rupert was my cousin. It turns out I was to sell penny stocks, highly speculative stocks, which were valued at under a dollar.

Once my license was under my belt, I was handed a phonebook and expected to call as many as a 100 people a day.

My fellow brokers and I spent the first two weeks of every month (8:30 to 5:00, and then again from 7:00 to 9:00) setting up prospects with cold calls. The script went like this, "Hi, I'm Ward Garner, and I work for XYZ Company. We sell stocks. I'm not here to sell you anything today. I'm doing business in your area and I just want to know if something good comes along, would you appreciate a call?"

On the third week of each month, we called back with "deals." On the fourth week, we picked up checks and went to the bank. It wasn't long before I was working in conflict with my own values and having trouble sleeping at night. I was making money but didn't feel good about myself.

During my first few months on the job, some newer brokers and I tried to sell mutual funds, a safer investment. The company owners, on the other hand, pressured us to push the crappy penny stocks. They justified the practice by claiming that the individuals who bought the stocks would throw their money away in any case. So why shouldn't we get a commission?

By September, after a few months on the job as a penny stockbroker, I found myself enduring even more sleepless nights and feeling the need to resign. In fact, I had become a swindler. To make matters worse, I had invested time and money into becoming a licensed stockbroker. I was 28 and stuck.

Looking back, I still feel sick to my stomach about my days as a penny stockbroker. At the time, the experience was devastating. I felt betrayed by Rupert and stupid for not seeing the penny stockbroker situation for what it was. The newer brokers were simply workhorses for the company, viewed as dumbass sales guys.

The desire for success and fancy things had blurred the lines between right and wrong for me. The desire distorted my good values. An overly trusting nature had kept me from asking questions and seeing an unethical situation for what it was. Thankfully, I was saved by the lack of a good night's sleep.

In October 1990, I was unemployed and not sleeping for an entirely different reason. It was scary, especially given how much I had invested to get my license. I had jumped in with both feet and rented an apartment with another new broker on Mt. Washington, a fancy section of the city. Yet another taste of reality came when my roommate's Jaguar was repossessed. The lines of good sense and morality had blurred for him as well.

Thankfully, I did have the stockbroker's license and had maintained a clean record. I was able to secure an entry-level position at a boutique money management firm. I was nervous about taking this new job but needed an income. Thankfully, at this new job, I learned the difference between a stockbroker and a fiduciary.

A stockbroker is a salesperson who earns a commission on what he or she sells. A fiduciary is an individual in whom another places the utmost trust to manage and protect property or money. The fiduciary relationship is one of trust in which one person has a moral, ethical, and legal obligation to act for another's benefit. Typically, a fiduciary prudently takes care of money for another person.

Think of a fiduciary relationship as one in which one party is obligated to put the other party's interest ahead of his or her own in every financial transaction.

A fiduciary charges a fee rather than a commission; this is typically a one percent fee based upon assets, charged quarterly. Thus, the fiduciary doesn't struggle with an inherent financial conflict the way a commissioned stockbroker naturally does.

I happily became a fiduciary—no longer just a salesperson. I was selling a full service, rather than a product. After the initial sale, 100% of my talents could go to work for the client. This became my life's work. Today, as a fiduciary, I offer management meetings, advice, whole picture assessments, etc. The work goes beyond dollars and cents. My goal in life is to help people, not make my living at their expense. I've been sleeping well at night for years.

Now, with 25 years in the role of fiduciary as a registered investment advisor, I remain shaped by my negative experience as a penny stockbroker. I had been swindled into becoming a swindler! Since the day I woke up to this fact, I've been forever vigilant against the swindle—whether against my clients or myself. Call me a cynic, but I believe if you have money, you are a swindler's target.

I've worked with hundreds of people with complex financial situations and experiences and heard enough stories to fill a number of books. In the process, I've learned that the swindle is neither as obvious nor as simple as it might seem at first. I've written this book to share what I learned along the way.

If you are in your senior years and have a high net worth, you've obviously managed to beat many swindles along the way. Congratulations. This doesn't mean you are safely out of the woods. In fact, the more money you have, the more others will look to you to meet their needs, whether those needs are your legitimate concern or not.

When you have money, you have to navigate your way through a sea of people who want you to pay them for advice or services. You also have to navigate your way through waves of requests from your children (especially the adult ones), relatives, and causes. And, having made it safely so far, you are likely to be at risk from the storm of your own ego and the needs surrounding longevity.

The material in this book will help you consider each of these elements with fresh eyes and keep navigating successfully. In short, even if you know a lot about building and maintaining wealth, this book will help you stay on track. I wrote this book with you in mind.

If you are younger and just building your net worth, this book is for you, too. The chapters contain straightforward advice and cautionary tales to help you make good financial decisions, the kind that grow money rather than deplete it. One of my primary goals in this book is to protect you from the swindle and other threats to your financial well-being. With the average lifespan stretching its way toward 100, you'll want to be sure you have the assets you need as you age.

If you are in the position of having inherited wealth that you must now preserve and grow, this book is for you as well. You face a great deal of pressure and may not feel confident you have the tools to make the best of what's been left to you. You, too, must protect yourself from the swindle and other threats to your net worth. You, too, must plan for retirement and the passing of your wealth to the next generation. Keep this book nearby as you make your way.

WHAT TO EXPECT FROM THIS BOOK

This book is a series of practical chapters full of information and tips to guide you to good decisions for financial health. While each chapter can stand alone, they are arranged in the following themes:

1. If you have money, you are the target of intentional and unintentional swindles.

2. If you have any family at all, your money is vulnerable to the complexities of love and loyalties.

3. If you are subject to the same realities of life as everyone else, you've got to protect your money.

4. If you are human, you pose a risk to your own financial security.

It may seem like I have a negative approach to financial security. Perhaps I do. I freely admit that I've been influenced permanently by my brief experience as a penny stockbroker. From that experience, I learned that even people with good intentions can be misguided and/or conflicted. I also learned that it's not that tough to dupe another human being—or to dupe yourself.

I might simply think of myself as cynic when it comes to the trustworthiness of financial advice, except for the experiences I've had over 25 years as a fiduciary. I've seen smart people make bad decisions, parents threaten their own security to take responsibility for adult children, people lose large parts of estates unnecessarily to taxes, and well-meaning neighbors urge others to buy products from swindlers. Perhaps I'm more of a realist than a cynic.

How about if you read the chapters and decide for yourself? Whether you decide I'm a cynic or a realist, you'll learn valuable information and tips that will help you build your own wealth.

Let's get started!

SECTION 1

IF YOU HAVE MONEY,
YOU ARE THE TARGET OF A SWINDLER

THE STORY OF HOW I GOT SWINDLED into being a swindler is a cautionary tale. I'm not suggesting someone will trick you into becoming a penny stock-broker who deceives innocent people into putting their savings into highly speculative stocks. I don't see that as a real danger.

On the other hand, in the busy pace of life, we are often blind to experiences and encounters that cost us money unnecessarily. Sometimes the cost is tiny and sometimes it's not. Often, one person's honest way of making a living is an unintentional swindle against another.

At other times, even our elementary school kids try to manipulate and swindle us for trendy toys or designer clothes. We don't think of our kids as swindlers, simply as kids who respond to impulse and peer pressure. If you give in often enough, your bank account balance will fall noticeably.

And let's face it: Sometimes we swindle ourselves. The range for the self-swindle is broad, from rationalizing a big purchase to risking all of our money on a get-rich-quick promise.

The chapters in the first section of this book all focus on identifying various swindles and taking steps to protect yourself from them. These chapters lay a foundation and introduce themes that I'll cover in more detail throughout the book. I'll touch on the lure that comes with unrealistic promises, give some advice on protecting yourself from paying unnecessary taxes, and, most importantly, remind you that the word "No" is most often your best defense against a declining net worth.

CHAPTER 1

KNOW THE SOURCES OF THE SWINDLE:
THE OBVIOUS AND NOT SO OBVIOUS

I F YOU HAVE MONEY, YOU ARE ON THE SWINDLER'S LIST, and you need to be on guard. This is not as easy as it might seem, because a swindler can be anyone from a Bernie Madoff clone, to a penny stockbroker, to a teenager behind the counter at a big box store. In some ways, the teenager is the most dangerous because the kid is an unintentional swindler.

Chances are you learned the dictionary definition of a swindler long ago. Even so, let's take a brief look at the various types of swindlers you will surely encounter. I want to make the case that many swindles are so subtle you don't even see them coming. In fact, sometimes you are simultaneously your own swindler and victim.

INTENTIONAL SWINDLER
The classic swindler is a charlatan, a person practicing quackery, fraud, or a similar confidence trick in order to get your money, property, or advantage by pretense. The intentional swindler is the type of person who outwardly communicates that he or she only has your best interests at heart.

Intentional swindlers go to extraordinary means to prove they are credible and trustworthy. They do not come with signs above their heads warning potential victims of their prowls. No, intentional swindlers look, sound, and act like the real deal. Often they promote their hard work and brag about each of their honest endeavors, however small. With the passage of time, the whole truth comes out.

For example, Alan Stanford, a real estate tycoon, started Stanford International Bank Limited in 1986, an affiliate of Stanford Financial Group. It's hard for me to forget the question posed to billionaire Alan Stanford on a CNBC show around that time: How does it feel to be a billionaire?

With confidence and an air of credibility, Stanford replied, "It feels real good to be a billionaire."

A short time after his final interview in 2008, Stanford was charged and later convicted in connection with the bank's $8 billion dollar billion investment scheme that offered ridiculous and unjustified high interest rates. Stanford International Bank Limited offered Certificates of Deposit at rates consistently higher than those available from banks in the United States. It was just another Ponzi scheme.

Intentional swindlers, like Stanford, are consummate charmers and liars. The script I was given in my penny stock misadventure was meant to charm people on the phone. The cold calls we made in the first two weeks of every month were designed to disarm, build trust, and make an unrealistic promise seem true. In the third week, we followed up with the "deal," the swindle. During the fourth week, we cashed in. It was a classic swindle that still makes me sick to think about.

Upon discovery that they've been conned, victims of an intentional swindle express shock and surprise. The swindler seemed sincere and trustworthy. When the swindler completes his or her task, not only is the victim's net worth lost, so is his or her pride. It feels horrible to be duped.

You might think you are too smart for this kind of swindle. Watching the evening news on a regular basis convinces me otherwise. People from all occupations, all education levels, and all financial situations routinely lose their life savings to a swindler. The best advantage you can give swindlers is to believe you are immune. The best advantage you can give to yourself is to know you are not immune.

FINANCIAL PRODUCT SALESPERSON

Anyone who gets a commission for selling a financial product is a type of swindler, whether intentional or not. With the opportunity for commission comes a built-in conflict of interest. The salesperson needs to put food on the table, whether or not the product is right for you. Even if that salesperson believes in the product, he or she could be selling you something that you don't need.

For example, consider a salesperson trying to convince you to buy whole life insurance. The purpose of whole life insurance is to allow you to provide for your family in the event of your death. The premiums you pay for this security also accumulate a cash value.

Emotions, as well as practical considerations, surround the purchase of life insurance. The salesperson will lead you to believe that you will always need life insurance to protect your family. In fact, life insurance is expensive, and the need for it is a moving target.

Analyze the need for life insurance at each stage of your life, and you will find plenty of circumstances in which life insurance is unnecessary. Yes, the need to protect a young family in the case of a breadwinner's death is real. As your kids and you age, however, scenarios change.

For example, if your kids are grown, your need to spend down your assets is low, and (after 40 years of saving and investing) your net worth is substantial, you typically do not need life insurance. On the other hand, if your estate, as a single person, is over $5.25 million or, as a couple, is over $10.5 million, you might want life insurance so that your beneficiaries can use the proceeds for federal inheritance tax.

The salesperson will argue, "You might need life insurance later and be unable to buy it due to health-related reasons." Or, "Buy life insurance when you are young because it is cheaper." These are sales pitches. Don't let yourself be swindled by them. Purchase life insurance only when there is a specific purpose for it.

Whenever you interact with any financial salesperson, be aware of the built-in conflict of interest. Also, be aware that a financial salesperson is a specialist who is unqualified to give advice about your complete financial picture. Even if a specific product might be in your best interest, you should evaluate that product in light of your entire financial, tax, and estate picture.

UNINTENTIONAL SWINDLER

The world is replete with unintentional swindlers. These individuals are especially dangerous because they have no idea what they are doing.

Put yourself in this scenario: Your neighbor, golf buddy, or relative talks to you about a salesperson of whom he or she thinks highly. This is a case of a person you trust advising you to work with this person he or she trusts. You decide to check the recommendation out.

Perhaps the salesperson is an insurance agent, banker, accountant, or someone else. You end up buying a product from someone who, at best, has a limited perspective. In short, you put yourself at risk of working with a non-fiduciary because an unqualified advisor had a good feeling or experience with a salesperson. Anything can happen, even though your neighbor, golf buddy, or relative has only the best intentions.

Perhaps no swindler is as clueless of the swindle as a teenager behind the counter at a big box store. Here is how it works: When you purchase something from an electronics store that cost more than $100, the cashier asks if you would like to buy replacement insurance on the item. In my opinion, this is outrageous, and a swindle.

The seller has been given a script, just as I was when I became a penny stock sales broker. In this case, the teenager has incomplete or inexpert information. If the kid had knowledge about insurance and any ethics at all, he or she would advise you to insure against significant loss only, because everything else is a waste of money. A significant loss is anything that, if you needed to pay to replace it immediately, you may have to go without food for some period.

The party who sells nominal insurance on small electronics always has a script of why the insurance comes in handy. The explanation can make sense to the person walking with a cloud over his or her head. Don't be this person!

SELF OR LOVED ONE SWINDLER

Among the biggest swindles to which we are all vulnerable are the ones we perpetrate upon ourselves or within our families. Even though money involves numbers, it doesn't work objectively like math. Money is a complex issue that gets all tied up with family, emotions, love, loyalty, pride, and ego. Here are just a few examples.

We might find ourselves justifying the purchase of excessively expensive gifts for young kids because we feel guilty over divorce or long work hours. We might get stuck in enabling patterns with our adult children who struggle with irresponsibility or addiction. We might give yet another loan to a brother or cousin, believing this time will be different. We might accept big losses because we can't bring ourselves to trust anyone's advice but our own, even though we don't have time to do our own research.

I hope I've made my case that swindles present a real and present danger. Keep reading to delve more deeply into the dangers that lurk and discover steps to protect your wealth. This book is not just a cry of alarm; it's about solutions.

For now, however, remember the adage: If you have money, you are on the swindler's list. Heck, even if you only have funds enough to buy small electronics, you are on the list!

Be aware that intentional swindlers are typically subtle and likable people. Also, be aware that your trusted neighbor, golf buddy, or relative might be an unintentional swindler. Know the difference between a salesperson and a fiduciary. And be honest about the fact that sometimes you and/or a loved one can be a threat to your wealth. Awareness is the first positive step. Keep reading!

CHAPTER 2

BE WARY OF ANY PROMISE
NOT GROUNDED IN REALITY

C HANCES ARE YOU ARE FAMILIAR with at least the outlines of the story of Bernie Madoff, first class swindler. Currently serving a jail term of 150 years, he forfeited $17.179 billion dollars. Arrested in 2008, Madoff claimed that he started his Ponzi scheme in the 1990s. Investigators think it might have been even earlier. How did Madoff get away with this scheme for so long? How did he defraud thousands of investors in the process? How is it that his group of victims included large endowments, banks, and people with great academic achievement?

You need to know the answer to this question because a similar thing could happen to you, even if you are smart and well informed. Imagine, for instance, you are just beginning to manage an endowment fund that has been in your family for generations. You've been introduced to a money manager of a very selective firm, a large firm with billions of assets under management. If any of the following things happen to you, beware. You might be the target of an intentional swindle of the Bernie Madoff variety.

EVERYTHING IS ARRANGED TO MAKE
YOU FEEL SPECIAL

From the first moment you walk into the intentional swindler's office, you experience the wow factor. No detail is left to chance. The sights, sounds, and attention leave you overwhelmed. Moreover, you feel as if you have found the elusive place where heaven meets earth.

The offices are exceptional. The location is exclusive, and the furnishings are of the highest caliber. Nothing but the top name brands. Exclusivity is key, the more exclusive the better. The level of fine finish is first class, and the service is five stars.

When you are greeted in the formal reception area, the voice you hear is sophisticated and formal. You are left unattended briefly, but there is never enough time for you to take it all in. The sights and sounds are magical. It's overwhelming.

The goal of the swindler, on one hand, is to convey the feeling, with ambiance and service, that "you have arrived." On the other hand, and more important, the swindler wants to convey the feeling that you deserve this above-average treatment. Such treatment is not available to those of a lessor vintage. The décor and service creates the necessary illusion, that you are worthy of higher rates of return that are reserved for special people like you.

YOU ARE PROMISED UNREALISTIC RETURNS

You are informed that you will receive an above-average return, to the tune of 20%, every year. Furthermore, you are told you needn't worry about loss of capital because you are now working with "the experts." There is some plausible explanation. For example, the swindler might say, "We do things this way to make your projections much easier. Variable rates of return just make planning too difficult."

The swindler's end game is always the same. The message: Just move your assets over here and wait for the money to roll in. Give us the money and relax. Just make your projections. Your loved ones are counting on you.

YOU ARE ASSURED THAT THIS FIRM IS SMARTER THAN OTHER FIRMS

You learn that, given this firm's highly skilled traders, you will never be invested when the market is going down. You will never suffer a loss. Beware of unrealistic promises.

Once you are engaged with a swindler, you're in a battle with your senses. Your first sense is that this doesn't seem right. Your second sense is that the promise does not seem possible. Your third sense argues that if the promised returns weren't possible, the company would have gone out of business by now. Just look at how nice their offices are.

So how did Bernie Madoff do it? Simple, he made his clients feel special. When you feel special, reality matters less.

Face it: No matter how special you may be, you can't have something that does not exist. If normal rates of return are 10% for stocks, unless you are clear about how you will end up with 20% rates of return, don't pursue it. You are being swindled.

Beware of special treatment. Consider time your friend. Do not make sudden moves with your money. Instead, take your time and rely on your senses and intuition. Seek to understand fully how decisions are made and how the results are obtained. If a promise sounds too good to be true, ask more questions. If it seems that some form of voodoo is involved in getting results, don't walk away—run!

CHAPTER 3

KEEP THE TAX SWINDLE IN CHECK

O N FEBRUARY 3, 1913, the Sixteenth Amendment to the Constitution of the United States allowed Congress to apply an income tax without restriction. Franklin D. Roosevelt later said, "Paying tax is a privilege of membership in an organized society."

Ronald Reagan, famous for insisting we have high taxes because we overspend, said, "Government's view of the economy could be summed up in a few short phrases: If it moves, tax it. If it keeps moving, regulate it. And if it stops moving, subsidize it." He also quipped, "A taxpayer is someone who works for the federal government but doesn't have to take the civil service examination."

The government is definitely out for your money, especially any inherited money—but there are things you can do to reduce the amount taken. Follow these steps to pursue your right to pay the least amount of taxes.

DETACH YOURSELF EMOTIONALLY FROM TAX SITUATIONS

Always give yourself space to think about tax payments logically. For example, imagine you receive a tax notice from the Internal Revenue Service (IRS). The letter states that you sold 1,000 shares of Heinz stock, amounting to $42,000. The IRS says you owe, $6,300, plus late payment penalties and interest.

You don't recall selling the stock. In fact, the Heinz Company was sold even though you voted against it. You simply received a check. Is it your fault for not telling the accountant?

A quick reaction to the IRS can be a costly mistake, so don't respond to this situation by writing a check. Instead, realize that you must have paid some amount of money for the Heinz stock shares originally; this is your original cost basis. If the original purchase price were $5 per share, your basis would be $5,000. At the very least, a quick call to the IRS can help you get the facts you need to proceed.

Your proceeds, less your original basis, are equal to the taxable amount for the calculation of capital gain tax. In this example, the proceeds for the transaction were $42,000, and the original cost basis was $5,000, so the capital gain tax is based upon a $37,000 gain, not $42,000. Taking a step back and figuring out the cost basis will save you $750, or 15% of $5,000.

If you inherited the Heinz stock, you will owe capital gain tax on the amount over your stepped-up basis. A stepped-up basis is equal to the average value of the stock on the date of death. This is determined by adding the stock's low and high price for the day, then dividing it by 2. So, if the high was $6 and the low was $4 on the day of the death, the average price would be $5.

It's easy to get emotional when receiving a tax bill—or even when thinking of the tax impact of any financial decision. Always take a step back, get the facts, and act accordingly. As appropriate, get professional help.

BE MINDFUL OF YOUR TAX BRACKET WHEN MAKING FINANCIAL DECISIONS

Our progressive tax system means that the more you make, the higher the tax bracket or percentage the government will take from your earnings. As you make decisions about liquidating investments and taking IRA distributions, be mindful of the impact on your tax bracket.

For example, imagine an elderly woman with a low income inherits several hundred thousand dollars from her deceased brother in the form of an IRA. It is in stocks, bonds, and mutual funds. The woman hears on the radio that the market is going south, so she calls up the financial advisor and says, "Sell everything and send me a check."

Assuming the financial advisor is unable to dissuade her, here are the results of her decision: She was in the zero tax bracket because her income, once her personal exemption and standard deduction were taken into account, was below the taxable amount. Now that she has taken the entire IRA in the form of a check, her income is north of $400,000. That means she will owe tax of approximately $118,000 plus 39.6% of the amount over the amount of $400,000.

The woman would have saved a great deal if she had made a plan for withdrawal. To reduce her exposure to the stock market, she could have done so within the IRA by changing the ratios. She did not need to take the money out of the IRA to protect it. Had she taken the distribution over several years, she would have paid far less tax.

Pursue your right to pay the least amount in tax because it is your right. The government will not help you in this regard. They are conflicted. They work for the taxpayer, but there is never enough money to fund the government properly, so why would they help you pay less? Only you can insist on paying the least amount of tax.

ITEMIZE YOUR DEDUCTIONS

Don't fall for the myth claiming that itemizing your deductions will earn you an IRS audit. The federal tax code is based upon the honor system. If you have a deduction, take it. Make the effort every year to prepare your tax report in a manner that allows you to pay the least amount. This is your right.

ACCEPT THE REALITIES OF SOCIAL SECURITY

The biggest government swindle of all is Social Security. Why? Most people are taxed twice on the same money. When President Franklin D. Roosevelt signed the legislation that created Social Security, the benefits were not to be taxable. Today, for most people, this is not the case. Today, the reward for saving and investing is paying more tax; sometimes we pay tax twice on the same money. Social Security is one such instance.

According to the Internal Revenue Service, a quick way to find out if any of your benefits may be taxable is to add one-half of your Social Security benefits to all your other income, including any tax-exempt interest. Next, compare this total to the base amounts below. If your total is more than the base amount for your filing status, then some of your benefits may be taxable. In 2015, three base amounts are as follows:

1. $25,000
   For single, head of household, qualifying widow or widower with a dependent child or married individuals filing separately who did not live with their spouse at any time during the year.

2. $32,000
   For married couples filing jointly.

3. $0
   For married persons filing separately who lived together at any time during the year.

If it is not possible to keep your taxable retirement income below the levels of taxation outlined above, don't spend your energy complaining about it. Instead, be happy that you have a substantial income.

PREPARE FOR THE RESPONSIBILITY OF SUDDEN WEALTH

The best of all possible outcomes, when preparing for the receipt of significant wealth, is to be prepared both intellectually and emotionally. If you are a spouse or an adult child likely to inherit, don't wait until a death to prepare for the transfer of wealth. Although you may find it difficult to talk about death and money, failing to do so can result in unnecessary distress and loss of your wealth. If it is at all possible, communicate openly and even participate in developing the plan to transfer wealth.

Here are other steps you can take to be well prepared for inherited wealth:

1. Understand Business Concepts and the Capital Markets
   Whether you expect to inherit or not, you owe it to yourself to understand how investment in the capital markets work. You also need to understand general business concepts, such as accounting and taxation. The more you learn before the transfer of wealth, the better decisions you will make when you have the money.

2. Understand and Stick to the Wealth Transfer Plan
   The transfer of family wealth is difficult and wrought with emotion. You may or may not agree with the transfer plan established by your benefactor. However, you'll need to follow the plan that was set into motion at the death of a loved one in order to obtain maximum tax savings at the time of transfer. Be sure to understand the objective and implementation steps of the transfer plan. Get the family attorney involved. Listen and stick to the plan. However, listen to your logic and intuition; if things don't seem to add up, get a second opinion.

3. Work with a Financial Advisor in a Fiduciary Relationship
   Few people are both extremely objective and knowledgeable about the capital markets, especially when their own money is at risk. So hire an objective professional. Depending on your skill set,

desire, and the amount of wealth, you will need a financial advisor, attorney, and an accountant. Each has a particular skill set necessary to manage wealth.

4. Develop an Investment Policy Statement
   An Investment Policy Statement is a document outlining the goals, objectives, and risk parameters used in the management of wealth. This helps you to communicate clearly with your advisors.

5. Take Advantage of the Step-Up in Basis Due to Death
   The general rule applied to property received from a benefactor is that the beneficiary's basis equals the fair market value of the property at the time the decedent dies. You can take advantage of the step-up in basis to reallocate a portfolio of stocks, bonds, and real estate to meet your goals and objectives. With a step-up in basis, you can sell assets with little or no capital gain tax.

6. Take Required Beneficiary IRA Distributions
   These are often called beneficiary required minimum distributions or Beneficiary RMDs. The penalties for not taking Beneficiary RMDs are significant. If less than the death RMD amount is distributed, the beneficiary may be subject to a 50% excess accumulation penalty on the amount of the shortfall.

Chapter 4

Learn How to Say No

N O MATTER YOUR CURRENT NET WORTH, it will grow or shrink in relation to your commitment to the word, *no*. If you want your net worth to grow, learn to say no in the following categories.

Say No to Overindulging Your Wants

Learn to make the distinction between wants and needs. Our society encourages us to buy when the urge strikes, whether we need the item or not. It seems as though everyone around us is buying and indulging in superficial toys and experiences. We come to think we have a right to indulge in our urges to buy, travel, and consume. After all, advertising messages tell us we deserve it. This mentality is so pervasive that it can feel embarrassing not to keep up—with vacations, cars, designer clothes, technological toys, etc.

In fact, you either learn how to say no to things you don't need—or watch your net worth decrease as your money continually disappears. You might find yourself unable to pay for a service or product you genuinely need.

We all have limited resources, so being able to discern needs from wants is critical. Just say no to unnecessary spending, especially when your income will not support it.

I don't mean to say you shouldn't enjoy the life you've earned. I do mean to say that if you want your wealth to grow, you have to keep your urges to buy in check. And whatever you do, refuse the temptation to finance your wants on credit. That's a sure path to financial ruin.

Separating wants from needs not only protects your wealth, it provides an indispensable role model for your kids. Preaching won't work; demonstrating will.

SAY NO—OR AT LEAST PAUSE—WHEN YOUR KIDS PULL ON YOUR HEARTSTRINGS

Start early with role modeling and guiding children to distinguish between wants and needs. While it's natural for parents to want to give comfort and blessing to their children, it's easy to overdo it.

Young kids want, want, and want more. They are vulnerable to advertising, comparisons, and impulsivity. They will pull on your heartstrings because you seem like a money machine to them. It's up to you to set reasonable financial limits. It's up to you to teach your kids to distinguish between wants and needs.

It's also up to you to make a distinction between loving your kids and giving gifts to buy affection. When things aren't perfect at home, due to divorce, death, childhood illness, or any number of things, it's easy to assuage guilt with gifts. Be brutally honest with yourself about this. Gifts do not solve complex problems, and they can't buy affection. They can, however, make you vulnerable to manipulation.

SAY NO TO CONTINUED FINANCIAL IMMATURITY

Develop a strategy to help your children to become increasingly financially independent with time. Neither you nor your child will win if that child becomes a financially dependent adult.

Start with an allowance. This sets limits and teaches your children about money while avoiding the negativity associated with saying no too much. By giving age-appropriate amounts to your children in regular intervals, you can monitor their spending habits. You give your children the opportunity to learn from mistakes with small amounts before they need to handle larger amounts. If your child asks for more money before the next allowance is due, you have a teachable moment. Use the moment to help your child grow, especially about understanding the difference between needs and wants.

Use savings accounts to demonstrate how avoiding the wants can pay dividends in the future.

SAY NO TO ADULT CHILDREN'S REQUEST FOR MONEY

The cost of failing to teach your children financial independence is high; it may even lead to your personal bankruptcy. Once you give in to the financial needs of your adult child, you can expect that adult will be back for more. An adult dependent child's need and requests for money will not stop until all of your money is gone.

When your money has disappeared, the request for credit will come next. This may continue until you can no longer make the payment and have food on the table.

So begin with the end in mind; teach your child how to become financially independent early in life. And say no to an adult child's request for money. If you are already in the habit of supporting an adult child, changing the pattern is not easy, but you can do it. Set and stick to limits, until the adult becomes independent.

SAY NO TO THE TEMPTATION TO DISPLAY YOUR WEALTH

Be careful about talking about and displaying your wealth. Conspicuous consumption can let people know that you have had success in life. Having your brothers, sisters, cousins, and distant relatives recognize your success can feel good, but it can lead to problems. Your display of success can let a relative know where to go when times are tough. Sob stories, real or fake, pull at your heartstrings and make it extremely hard to say no to requests for money.

SAY NO TO SERVICE PROVIDERS, AT LEAST EVERY FIVE YEARS

In today's world, loyalty to a business goes unrewarded. Current business models sound like, "Give discounts to the new people at the expense of the loyal people."

This is true with insurance, especially car insurance. You must move your car insurance every five years to maintain the most competitive pricing. Insurers know that people are naturally lazy and don't want to move their policies. However, you will protect your wealth by not overpaying for this product or service if you consider moving your insurance every five years. Examine all such relationships at least every five years.

SAY NO TO THE REAL ESTATE SWINDLE

As in other professions, most real estate agents are good and moral people. Unfortunately, the very nature of the real estate business involves a swindle—and you fall for it the minute you sign a listing or sales agreement. Here is how it works.

In order for you to get the full value of your property, as well as an agent to get his or her 7% commission, your property has to sell for 107% of its highest and best value. When the property doesn't sell at this high price, the real estate agent will advise you to reduce the price.

Chances are that when your listing real estate agent finally presents an offer—perhaps at 80% of your asking (already reduced) price, you will have to weigh the benefits of selling far below your expected price versus bearing the cost of continuing to maintain the property. Chances are the realtor won't reduce his or her commission because the 7% is shared with another agent.

In a different scenario, the real estate agent may become the agent for both you (the seller) and the buyer (the people whose offer you are accepting). The listing real estate agent now also represents the buyer and becomes a dual agent. You must agree to a "dual agency with the same agent."

A dual agent cannot operate in a fiduciary capacity with either the seller or the buyer and must treat both equally. It is difficult, if not impossible, to obtain the highest and best price for the seller when the agent is also representing the buyer. Can you see the swindle here?

Protect yourself from the swindles inherent in working with a full-service real estate agent, especially the "dual agency with the same agency" scenario. You don't need a realtor to sell your house for 80% of the list price.

Consider marketing your home yourself, with the support of an attorney or a transaction broker. This is much easier than you might expect. You can get an MLS listing for $99 to $199, and listing your home on Craig's List is free. Once you have a willing buyer, you can hire an attorney to do the closing.

A transaction broker can perform a variety of services. For example, the broker can help the buyer prepare an offer for purchase, assist the seller in deciding what price to ask, facilitate communications between buyer and seller, write the contract, help the buyer and seller fulfill the conditions of the contract, and facilitate closing. Although not legally responsible to the buyer or seller, transaction brokers obviously are required by law to act honestly and to exercise due care.

Section 2

Money Is a Complex Family Affair

WHETHER YOU GREW UP IN A FAMILY with lots of money or one with very little, you entered adulthood with an emotional history with money. That history came complete with values, biases, expectations, and even trauma. When you married and prepared to start a family, chances are you and your spouse did not put your full money histories on the table for discussion. Chances are that much of the ripple effect of your experiences surrounding money is unconscious—and the same is true of your spouse.

Add in-laws, extended family members, and kids into the equation—with all their hidden histories and attitudes. Money often becomes an explosive and dividing issue. Add alcoholism, divorce, illness, or any other family stress, and things just get more challenging.

The chapters in this section all address some aspect of money and family. They will help you clarify the values that will be the foundation of your family and suggest ways for you to teach responsibility to your growing children. These chapters will encourage you to make peace with yourself regarding the mistakes you've made surrounding your money and kids—because every parent makes mistakes. In short, these chapters will help you make good decisions surrounding your family and money, no matter what your circumstances.

CHAPTER 5

BUILD A VALUE FOUNDATION WITH YOUR SPOUSE OR PARTNER

MONEY IS REPORTEDLY THE #1 REASON FOR problems in marriage, and the #1 reason for divorce. Whether a couple is rolling in dough or can barely afford to put food on the table, money is a highly charged issue—and one that colors every day of every week.

The messages around money from our first families influence our attitude toward saving and spending; our tolerance for risk; our likelihood to use money to bribe or punish others; and more. These attitudes, combined with our actions, have a profound impact, for good or ill, on our children throughout their entire lives.

If you want financial heath and harmony with your spouse and kids, you'll have to work with your partner to define your values, work toward balance, and establish boundaries with your kids. Here are some suggestions to help you get on a firm footing surrounding money and values.

ANSWER THE DEEP QUESTIONS ABOUT MONEY WITH YOUR SPOUSE OR PARTNER

It's a mistake to assume that your partner shares your values surrounding money. It's also a mistake to assume that the money values you *were taught*—as well as the ones you *caught* in your childhood home—are the healthiest ones. Chances are that many of your own values are hidden in your unconscious mind. One of the greatest gifts you can give your marriage and children is to clarify and communicate your values around money.

Even if you've been in a relationship for decades, you can learn a great deal about your partner and build harmony by discussing the following questions:

1. What did your parents teach you about money? What values did you pick up directly and indirectly? When you take emotion out of the equation, do you embrace those same values?

2. What primary sources have influenced your views about money? For example, did a relative try to buy your affection with money; did a religious leader give instruction; or were your parents constantly fighting about money? Does anxiety over money linger for you?

3. What is the purpose of wealth? What responsibilities do wealthy individuals have to society? Is philanthropy an obligation, a privilege, or neither?

4. What level of financial risk is comfortable and uncomfortable to you?

5. What financial obligations do parents have toward their children and grandchildren? Do parents owe them private school fees or college tuition? Do parents owe their children an inheritance? What is the appropriate balance?

6. What are the best ways to teach children financial responsibility? For example, should children receive an allowance, earn an allowance, or get no allowance? Should children be responsible for car insurance and other expenses?

7. What financial responsibilities do parents have for their adult children?

8. What financial responsibilities do parents have for their grandchildren?

9. What percentage of wealth, if any, should be given away?

10. What is the right attitude toward retirement? Should you and your spouse retire early and enjoy life, or work as long as possible to save every dime you can?

These are not easy questions, but you'll learn a lot about yourself and your partner if you dig deep. Answering these questions is a good first step toward building a financially sound team.

COME TO SOME AGREEMENT ABOUT MONEY WITH YOUR SPOUSE OR PARTNER

It may not be easy to come to an agreement, but listening to each other's history and ideas about money can help you begin with a point of understanding and respect. Negotiate and compromise until you can come to an agreement or meet in the middle on the bigger decisions.

For example, come to an agreement about what percentage of your income will go to savings. Agree on what level of risk you will assume together, and make a plan to teach your children how to be financially responsible. Even if you struggle to agree on money values as a couple, send a unified message to your kids. Explain what you are doing and why.

INFORM AND INVOLVE BOTH PARTNERS IN MONEY DECISIONS

In some families, one partner makes the money decisions and handles the finances. Many of us grew up with this kind of model. Dad managed the money as part of his mission to take care of Mom.

Life doesn't work that way anymore, and, all things being equal, Mom is as capable of figuring out finances as Dad. Marriage is a partnership, and both partners need to be informed and involved in the bigger money issues and decisions. Otherwise, one partner has more control, and your children may see that as a power differential. Lack of information also leaves one partner vulnerable should the other die unexpectedly.

LIVE WITHIN YOUR MEANS

I've already addressed the importance of distinguishing between wants and needs. Set a realistic budget and agree to stick to that budget. Refuse to buy things you want on credit. Refuse to buy on impulse in ways that break the budget.

When you set and honor a realistic budget, you prevent all sorts of tension and quarrels. You set yourself up for financial health. Equally important, your kids see and *catch* this behavior. What an incredible gift to give your children.

BE INTENTIONAL WITH YOUR CONVERSATIONS ABOUT MONEY

If money was a taboo subject in your household growing up, but don't repeat this mistake. Have consistent, reoccurring discussions about money. Such conversations allow your children to learn from you. This doesn't mean you have to share everything. Just be intentional and age-appropriate.

Of course, you won't manage money perfectly, but that's okay. Your actions, words, and even your struggles communicate your values. Talk about your mistakes as well as your successes with your kids.

Explain how much things cost and try to attach a value. For example, "Sally, here is a new baseball glove. It costs $58. I had to work nearly three hours for this glove at $20 per hour." Or, "This used car costs $18,000 and I make $56,000. That is one third of my annual income. I would have liked to have bought a new car, but we have other bills to pay as well." As kids get older, consider sharing your family budget with them.

Keep in mind that your children will learn dysfunctional lessons about money from outside sources. The education your children receive about money in school will be incomplete, inconsistent, and, at worst, detrimental. The education your children receive from television, media, and peers will certainly be detrimental. Make sure the money messages within your family are healthy and consistent.

TEACH AND MODEL GRATITUDE

In a culture in which nearly every message shouts, "You'll never be happy until you get more stuff," create a family culture in which you express gratitude for what you have. Consider making *thanksgiving* a daily tradition at dinner. Your kids will learn from your traditions as well as from your words and actions.

Consider encouraging a gratitude perspective by involving your kids in community service, fundraising, and philanthropy in age-appropriate ways.

LOOK AT THE REASONS BEHIND YOUR SPENDING

Families get bruised and broken in many ways, including divorce, illness, job pressures, and more. It's easy to get sucked into using money as a fix-it or as a weapon.

Don't allow yourself to attempt to buy affection from a child or to give expensive gifts to make up for losses. These strategies don't work, and they can encourage a child to be manipulative. On the other hand, don't withhold money from a child because he or she doesn't please you.

Don't allow yourself to enable an adult child because you don't want to face the truth about that child's addiction or other serious problem.

You can't solve emotional problems with money. You hurt everyone involved when you try. Take a hard look at your spending habits, especially when they surround painful family relationships and/or adult children.

Money is a complex family issue. None of us ever gets it exactly right. Even so, by building a family value structure with your partner, you give yourself and your children a solid foundation upon which to build. Your family value structure is a living thing. You can negotiate and renegotiate when life circumstances change. The most important thing is to listen to each other, agree on values, and communicate often.

.

CHAPTER 6

INSIST YOUR KIDS TAKE RESPONSIBILITY

THE TASK OF PARENTS IS TO PREPARE THEIR CHILDREN for adulthood. We need to send our kids out into the world with values, skills, self-confidence, and responsibility. A successful adult is one who *launches* and *accepts responsibility* for managing his or her own life.

If we want our kids to grow into financially responsible adults, we need to teach them responsibility as both a skill and a life attitude. Responsibility isn't just completing a task or paying a bill. It's also about an attitude, the idea of taking action, and being proud of doing it. It's the feeling you get from doing the right thing, at the right time, on your own. Like all other aspects of child rearing, teaching this is hard work. Here are some ideas for raising responsible kids.

START EARLY

From the earliest days, build a culture of helpfulness. Otherwise, you'll find yourself suddenly expecting a teenager to be responsible. Young children want to help, and you have many opportunities to reward helpful and responsible behavior. Ask a toddler to put his or her cup in the sink when finished.

Participate with your toddler in putting one activity away before taking a new one out. Make chores fun.

TEACH FIRST, AND THEN EXPECT YOUR KIDS TO BE RESPONSIBLE

For example, show your children how to make their beds, and then let them know you expect them to do it henceforth. Show them how to make snacks and sandwiches, and then explain that they should know how to do it henceforth. Install a clothes hamper in your children's rooms and let them know what you expect going forward.

Be careful to let your kids be kids and grow their skills. Avoid criticizing and correcting your kids when they don't do a task as neatly as you. The goal is to teach and reward responsibility, not demand perfection. Consistent harsh criticism can create rebellion.

BE RESPONSIBLE; EXPECT RESPONSIBILITY

If you don't demonstrate responsibility in your family, it's unrealistic to expect your kids to act responsibly. Your kids want structure and the attention that comes with accountability, but every child has built-in radar for hypocrisy. Make sure your behavior matches your words.

Childrearing books provide lists of age-appropriate chores and healthy options for rewarding the behaviors. You don't have to go overboard with rewards; in fact, big rewards lead to big demands and even a sense of entitlement. Kids naturally want to help contribute to the family. Chores lead to a sense of ownership. With ownership, pride can flourish.

Pride can lead to a positive attitude, and then initiative can flourish too.

As kids grow in responsibility, they will make mistakes. Create a family culture in which parents are approachable and mistakes are learning opportunities.

STRUCTURE AND ROUTINE ARE INVALUABLE

Children need structure and routine. Instead of offering rewards to get them to do chores, end the routine with a favorite activity. For example, if the favorite activity is watching television, set up the routine to clean up after dinner, then complete homework, and then watch television. The favorite activity comes at the end of the routine. Set up routines for school days/nights and non-school days/ nights.

ALLOW CONSEQUENCES TO TEACH RESPONSIBILITY

Every behavior in life has its consequences, good or bad. Help your kids learn this gradually. If they learn consequences when they make small bad choices growing up, they will be better prepared to make positive big choices when they leave home.

Help your children by allowing natural consequences to teach lessons. For example, if your child forgets his or her athletic gear, the child doesn't get to participate in athletic activities that day. Refrain from obstructing the natural consequences in such situations. Don't rescue your child by bringing the athletic gear, unless you want to do it often. Why should a kid remember, when there is little or no consequence?

When you set consequences and standards of behavior in your household, be consistent. For example, if the consequence for failing to do homework is an evening without a favorite television show, stick to that consequence even if you've had a bad day and don't want to hear the complaining that comes with the consequence.

REFUSE TO ACCEPT EXCUSES OR BLAMING BEHAVIOR

If your kid blames other people, places, or things for not meeting responsibilities or completing tasks, don't buy into it. Use examples from movies, the news, and experiences to talk about the fact that individuals always have choices and need to own up to their own behaviors. Refuse to accept explanations that make your kids into self-proclaimed victims.

HELP YOUR KIDS DEVELOP MONEY MANAGEMENT SKILLS

Allow your children to manage age-appropriate amounts of money and experience the consequences of their decisions. Demonstrate and set up opportunities for your children to experience the consequences of earning, saving, and spending.

As your child matures, consider increasing their responsibility by giving them more spending money. For example, you might give your teenager an allowance each fall to buy school supplies. Let your younger teenager be responsible for a clothing budget and your older teenager for all the related expenses, including clothing, school supplies, and equipment.

ENCOURAGE YOUR KIDS TO BE ENTREPRENEURS

Whether they want to sell lemonade, win prizes for school fundraising projects, or start a lawn mowing service, encourage your kids to set realistic plans and follow through with them. There is no better way to learn about money than to make and spend it on your own.

As your children get older, teach them more and more about entrepreneurship and financial realities. Help them to understand how synergies work in business. Talk about the business models you see in enterprises your family patronizes. Demonstrate the power of savings and compound interest. Teach kids how the stock market works; even give them some money to invest as a learning experience. Make financial decisions and lessons a part of your daily lives.

Being a parent is not easy; teaching responsibility, financially and otherwise, is tough, especially when you know you aren't always perfect in your own behaviors and decisions. Insisting your kids take responsibility, no matter how difficult, lays the groundwork for their own success in life. You owe them that—much more than you owe them a pair of designer sneakers. Give your kids the greater gift.

Chapter 7

Stand Tough in the Face of Manipulation

Young children naturally experiment with manipulating their parents. They know they are cute and that their parents love them; moreover, they sense their parents' discomfort in saying "no" to their youngsters. Kids naturally use their charms and strengths to get their way. If your child is building skills as a master of manipulation, beware. The worst is yet to come.

What might be cute in a young child can be upsetting and even dysfunctional in a teenager or adult. Many parents get trapped into giving in to manipulative behavior in their adult children. If you don't want to find yourself in this situation, understand and stop behavior in age-appropriate ways. If you are already in this situation, take action now.

Manipulation is a learned behavior—and it can be unlearned. Two immutable laws surround manipulative behavior.

1. If you reward the behavior, you'll get more of it.

2. Kids can only manipulate us if we permit them to. It takes two to tango.

Here are ideas you can use to stop the pattern of manipulation.

ACCEPT THE NATURE OF THINGS

Naturally, your child will go after what he or she wants in life. This is how humans learn to strategize. Be understanding of your child's desires, and then reward the behavior you desire. Punishing a child for manipulation tends to lead to more unwanted behavior. Ignoring behavior tends to extinguish it. Rewarding behavior, even with negative attention, reinforces it.

Reward your child for honesty and willingness to talk about his or her needs. Listen carefully, and then respond respectfully and thoughtfully.

KNOW THAT YOUR KIDS NEED AND WANT STRONG BOUNDARIES

While your kids may fight boundaries tooth and nail, at a deep level, they crave and need them. Think of structure and consistency as gifts you give your children.

STRIVE TO BE A PARENT RATHER THAN A FRIEND

It's not your job to ensure your child's happiness 100% of the time. Be alert for child manipulations based on happiness. For example, your child might try to hijack you emotionally by acting sad or angry until he or she acquires the desired object or activity.

Keep your focus on your role as a parent and your child's need for life skills. Insist the child act responsibly and take responsibility. Be firm in the face of manipulation.

BE AWARE OF YOUR OWN TRIGGERS

Children have an uncanny knack for knowing what, when, and how parents will react to certain behaviors and situations. Your child knows what makes you sad and exactly how to act to get a reaction from you. The act might be relentless begging, a tantrum, or something much more subtle. Your child knows how to use your reactions to his or her benefit.

Know what makes your blood boil and your tenderness rise. Recognize your reactions. This will help you to stay in control and build credibility with your child. Most important, it will allow you to see and stop manipulation in advance.

PRESENT A UNIFIED PARENTAL FRONT

When one parent regularly says "no" and the other says "yes," children certainly will play one parent against the other. This is learned behavior, so it can also be unlearned, but only if you and your spouse work together.

Agree to and stick to your bottom line as parents. Your kids will test your limits regularly and creatively. Manipulative behaviors are designed to throw you off your game and make you second-guess yourself. Be the parent, and stick to the established norms. If you have established guiding principles, repeat them often. Write and post your family's rules, so you don't get sucked into unproductive debates.

GIVE UNCONDITIONAL LOVE AND SUPPORT

Know that, in general, your children's desires and their pursuit of those desires have nothing to do with disrespect for you. They just want what they want, and they want to avoid what they do not want. It is that simple. You are just a parent caught up in the process. Stand firm against manipulation, but not against your child.

REWARD TRUTH-TELLING

Manipulation often comes in the form of half-truths and complete lies. By lying or failing to tell the full truth, kids withhold some degree of control from the parent. This allows the kids to get or do things that would not otherwise be possible, and there is the payoff. The only solution is to make sure lying doesn't work. Ever.

DON'T LET DIFFICULT LIFE CIRCUMSTANCES BREAK YOUR RESOLVE

Manipulation often gets worse in the face of difficult issues, such as divorce, illness, or loss of a job. Parents often develop a habit of compensating for guilty feelings over tough circumstances. This doesn't help the child and may lead to a sense of entitlement, which can be a lifelong problem. Deal with difficult circumstances by giving understanding and seeking professional help, not by giving stuff.

SAY "NO" TO KIDS WHO ASK YOU TO BAIL THEM OUT FINANCIALLY

Give your children opportunities to manage money and make mistakes in age-appropriate ways. Let them live and learn from the consequences of their mistakes. This is the only way for them to learn financial responsibility. While bailing your kids out may feel like a compassionate choice, it creates dependence.

If your child has grown into a person who habitually depends on you for cash, make it clear that you expect the behavior to stop. Then stick to your word. Unless you plan to live with your child and expect him or her to take good care of you throughout your senior years, keep your cash for retirement.

JOB DESCRIPTION

Job title: Parent every child wants and needs—no matter what that child says to the contrary!

Experience: Demonstrated leadership behavior

Skill sets:

1. Knows the difference between unconditional love and leniency

2. Sets and communicates firm boundaries

3. Has strong backbone—won't back down in the face of manipulation

4. Controls his or her emotional triggers—remains calm and consistent when the child test limits

5. Gives understanding instead of stuff—knows that money can't solve emotional problems

6. Insists the child builds personal responsibility, step by age-appropriate step

7. Models, teaches, and rewards honesty and hard work

8. Creates opportunities for the child to learn from age-appropriate experiences and mistakes

---

CHAPTER 8

MAKE PEACE WITH YOUR OWN MISTAKES SURROUNDING YOUR KIDS AND MONEY

I F YOU'VE MADE MISTAKES WITH YOUR KIDS, welcome to the club. Every parent makes mistakes, and many are tempted to wallow in guilt and regret over those mistakes. Often we try, consciously or unconsciously, to fix our mistakes with money or stuff. This can create a destructive spiral, leading to attitudes of entitlement and manipulative behavior in kids. Once this spiral gets started, it can have a paralyzing effect—making you believe it's too late to fix.

It is never too late to start over with kids and money; besides, the alternatives are lousy. You *can* regroup and start over, whether your kids are 10, 20, or 40. At any time, you can move from being passive about your kids and money to being active. Keep your chin up and read on.

Here are some common mistakes parents make with their kids, including suggestions for how to address them.

YOU HAVE A HABIT OF GIVING IN EASILY TO YOUR KIDS' WANTS

Parents make this mistake for a variety of reasons. Parents who didn't have much growing up naturally want their kids to have more. Other parents simply want to express their love, and their instinct is to do this with money or things.

It's never too late to set boundaries. For example, when your child demands an outrageously priced pair of designer shoes, you might talk about the distinction between wants and needs. Or you might give your child responsibility for a monthly or quarterly allowance for apparel. That way, your child gets to make choices within a budget and live with the consequences.

In any case, steel yourself for some drama and recognize that financial boundaries help your kids rather than hurt them. Delayed gratification can lead to better academic outcomes and fewer behavioral issues, as well as good financial decisions throughout life.

With immediate gratification, children who feel entitled can get confused when they become adults. Parents can then get stuck helping their kids into adulthood. It's never too late, however, to create boundaries and limits. It just gets harder as your kids get older.

YOU FEEL GUILTY FOR NOT PROVIDING A FREE RIDE TO THE BEST COLLEGE, EVEN THOUGH YOU CAN'T AFFORD IT

Many parents are willing to sacrifice so their children can go to Ivy League Schools, believing the old adage, "It isn't what you know, it's who you know." These parents fall into the trap of believing the best way to meet future well-to-do folks is to know them before they are rich and famous. Don't fall into this trap. The risk of overspending is certain, and the future reward is very uncertain. Not a good bet!

Always remember: Your kids can get student loans, but you can't get retirement loans. You have to be realistic. It's unwise to jeopardize your financial future for your child's college costs, especially without a guarantee.

Begin discussions about what types of colleges you can afford while your child is still years away from college. Clarify and communicate your values. While some parents feel it is their duty to send a debt-free child into the working world, others believe that college-age students need to learn financial responsibility by contributing. Kids who must contribute financially to their own education may take that education more seriously than those who don't. They also might make more of an effort to find and qualify for scholarships.

YOU REALIZE YOU'VE BEEN SPENDING SO MUCH TIME DEVELOPING YOUR CAREER THAT YOU'VE BEEN CHEATING YOUR KIDS OF TIME

While professional and monetary success is important, no success can compensate for failure in the home.

Your kids need you. There is no substitute for a parent. Lack of parent availability can contribute to problems with drugs, divorce, and worse. Nothing you can buy your children can compensate for the time you fail to spend with them.

If you've been making this mistake, make a change. It's not too late. Talk to your kids about what you've realized and how you are making a change.

YOU PRETEND TO YOUR KIDS THAT YOU ARE RICH WHEN YOU ARE REALLY STRUGGLING

If you have been deceiving your kids about money matters, it's time to stop. You may think that your money habits are private, but your kids can sense if things are good or not. If you have a heavy load of debt, chances are your household will be tense, anxious, and even argumentative.

Sit down and explain your reality to your kids in age-appropriate ways. While it would be inappropriate to burden your kids with your financial worries, they do need to be realistic about the standard of living your family can afford.

YOU NEVER TALKED ABOUT MONEY WITH YOUR YOUNG KIDS; NOW THEY SEEM TOO OLD FOR YOU TO BEGIN

Once again, it's never too late to make a change. Children, especially teenagers, are bombarded daily with society's financial values and habits. They need to hear from their parents, who are the most influential people in their lives.

Teaching your children about money and involving them in some family financial decisions can go a long way in helping them understand the value of money and the importance of the decision-making process. Ultimately, your kids will have to navigate these same waters when they become adults.

When your teenager wants something, don't just say, "That's too expensive," or, "We can't afford it." Help your child understand the other expenses that come with running a home and raising a family. If you feel comfortable, and it is age-appropriate, show the child your budget.

Encourage your children to help you plan family vacations so they can see just how expensive they are. When your kids participate in a vacation budget, they learn an important lesson—and they probably appreciate the trip more.

YOUR WEALTH IS DECREASING BECAUSE YOU'VE BEEN RESCUING YOUR ADULT CHILD FROM FINANCIAL IRRESPONSIBILITY

If you are in this position, you may feel stuck—and even ashamed. Once again, it's never too late to become active in changing the dynamic at play here. It won't be easy, but you owe this to your child and yourself. After all, you won't be here to take care of your adult child forever.

Consider talking to a counselor about your role, your partner's role, and your child's role in this dynamic. A professional can help you make a plan and stick to it.

Facing your mistakes about money and your kids is not easy, but there's no need to beat yourself up. Take a deep breath, face the facts, and make a change.

CHAPTER 9

PREPARE RESPONSIBLY FOR KIDS WITH SPECIAL NEEDS

P ARENTING A CHILD WITH SPECIAL NEEDS comes with a host of concerns. You need a carefully designed plan that ensures your child will always get the care he or she needs and deserves. Your plan must first address the years during which you are the child's guardian. It must also address the years during which your child will need a guardian after you pass on. Develop a comprehensive plan that will include lifetime supervision, maintenance of government benefits, management of funds, and funeral plans. Seek the advice of professionals who are specialists in providing services for families with special needs children. Here are some of the steps you'll want to take.

CREATE A SPECIAL NEEDS TRUST

This type of trust is designed for beneficiaries who are disabled, either physically or mentally. This special needs trust, a critical part of your child's long-term plan, will allow you to leverage public money. Be sure the trust is written so that the beneficiary can enjoy the use of property held in the trust for his or her benefit, while at the same time receiving essential needs-based government benefits.

Use the special needs trust to allocate savings and gifts given to your child. If you receive money from an insurance settlement for the child, deposit the money in the special needs trust. Make this trust the beneficiary of your personal life insurance policy. If your place of work provides life insurance, make the special needs trust the beneficiary there too. Finally, make the special needs trust the beneficiary of your estate, ensuring that those assets aren't passed to your child directly when you die.

MAKE A PLAN FOR YOUR CHILD'S LIFE IN ADULTHOOD

When your child reaches about 18 to 20 years old, a change in living arrangements may be appropriate. Investigate options and make plans earlier rather than later.

If your adult child will continue to live with you, identify the personnel you will need to compensate. Investigate the day programs for adults with special needs available in your area.

If independent living is the goal, investigate options in your community such as shared living, group homes, or apartments. Once you find a place you like, get on the waiting list ASAP.

DO YOUR BEST TO INCREASE SAVINGS

Children with special needs have many incidental expenses which are not covered by outside sources. For example, your health insurance may not cover all the therapies or treatments your child needs. Your school system may not offer the special training that is ideal for your child. In such cases, your personal savings are essential. Never put the earmarked money in your child's name. Use the special needs trust to protect the savings for the child.

Savings can also pay for a special needs advocate. A special needs advocate is an expert in special education who can help you with the paperwork, programs, and laws that affect what services your child receives. An advocate can ensure your child receives all the services he or she is entitled to from the local school district and community.

BECOME A LEGAL GUARDIAN

The age at which your special needs child is considered an adult by law, with the rights to make medical and financial decisions, varies by state. If your child is incapable of making such decisions, obtain legal guardianship for financial, legal, and healthcare affairs. This will allow you to maintain the same supervision and control you had over these as you did when your child was younger.

MAKE PLANS FOR YOUR ADULT CHILD AFTER YOUR DEATH

1. Create or Update Your Will
   Stipulate that your assets will be left to the special needs trust and not to your child. Hire a lawyer who works specifically for people with special needs.

2. Think in Terms of Checks and Balances
   Designate people to fill two distinct roles: successor guardian and successor trustee. By separating these roles, you ensure a checks and balances sys-

tem for your child's future needs. The last thing you need to worry about is fraud.

Your successor guardian is the person or entity who takes over and continues the role of the parental guardian after your death.

Tending to a child or adult with special needs is a time-consuming job. Ask yourself who can handle that type of commitment. Who has already bonded with your child? Who has the patience, understanding, and personality necessary to deal with the day-to-day responsibilities of your child with special needs?

Your successor trustee is the person or entity who steps in and takes full control of your special needs trust at the time of your death. The successor trustee can be a family member, friend, or even a bank or lawyer. The successor trustee is responsible to ensure that the money in the trust is spent only on your child with special needs and only on services that you've specified or that are appropriate to your child's needs.

The trustee is also to supervise how the money in the trust is invested. The successor guardian cannot spend any money in the trust without the trustee's approval.

3. Prepare for the Successor Guardian
    Prepare a schedule and a list of your child's preferences as well as a contact information worksheet. Write down your child's daily routine with as

much detail as possible. Do the same for your child's daily, weekly, and monthly schedules. Information regarding preferences provides invaluable guidance to the successor guardian and others who will support your special needs child.

Be sure to explain your specific wishes for daily care of your child, including your child's preferences for foods, activities, and music. Communicate your child's preferences for bathing, dressing, and toileting. Describe living situations that you believe will provide your child with security, dignity, and self-esteem. Describe your child's communication style and give guidance regarding how to interpret your child's words and behavior. Share your child's religious affiliation and your wishes for final arrangements.

Create a list of contact information for your child's physicians, therapists, and other medical support people, as well as current medications, dosages, and schedules. If there are individuals whom you don't want around your child or activities to avoid, write those down too.

CHAPTER 10

KEEP INHERITED ASSETS SEPARATE FROM MARRIAGE ASSETS

I MAGINE THIS SCENARIO: You have been married for 25 years, and your spouse looks as good to you as the day you married. The kids are grown and you are empty nesters. Out of the blue, you get the call that your dad has passed away. This is a shock, as your mom passed just a year earlier. You don't want to deal with the closing of your father's estate, but you are an only child, so you don't have a choice.

You and your spouse have shared financial accounts since the day you married. Accordingly, you take Dad's money—let's say it is $1 million—and put it into joint names. You include a Transfer On Death (TOD) designation, so the kids get the money when you and your spouse both pass.

Although comingling inherited property with marital property may seem like the reasonable and loyal thing to do, it can be a big mistake. It's good practice to segregate all inherited property from marital property. Here are three examples to explain why.

Exᴀᴍᴘʟᴇ #1

Out of nowhere, you catch your spouse cheating on you with a colleague. He or she asks for a divorce. Not only are you losing your spouse, you are unnecessarily losing half of what you inherited. The loss of one half of the money is due to your comingling of the inherited assets with your marital assets by holding them in joint name with your soon to be ex-spouse. Now you have to share the $1 million inheritance.

Like most people who comingle their inherited assets, you never thought it was possible for you to lose your spouse to an ugly divorce. Unfortunately, it happens.

Exᴀᴍᴘʟᴇ #2

You're successful, and your brother, who happens to be unmarried with no children, suddenly passes away. He leaves you his $1 million beach house. You and your spouse share the title on your current residence, so sharing the title on the beach house seems natural and normal. A few years later, your spouse unexpectedly files for divorce.

Your soon-to-be ex-spouse demands that the beach house be sold and one-half of the proceeds be awarded to him or her. Now you have to find the money to pay your spouse for half of the beach house or you'll be forced to sell it. The housing market is down, so it is not the ideal time to sell the house. Whether you sell or pay your spouse another way, you lose half of your inherited property unnecessarily.

Exᴀᴍᴘʟᴇ #3

Recently, your uncle passed away and left incredible gifts. Both you and your partner of many years love spending time in the $1 million ski chalet at Beaver Creek, Colorado. When your uncle died, you never thought twice about sharing his bounty with your partner. At 60 years old and childless, it was a no-brainer to put everything in joint name.

Unfortunately, your partner's gambling problem resurfaces after many years. You knew your partner had a problem prior to your relationship, but so much time has passed since then.

Your partner tells you about the problem. He or she owes more than $1 million for gambling losses. Your partner confesses to signing a loan to satisfy an online gambling debt. Now your partner can't make the loan payments—and cannot keep the creditors from foreclosing on the marital property. The ski chalet must be sold. Had you kept your inherited property separate from your marital property, the ski chalet would still be yours.

It may seem disloyal and pessimistic to insist upon keeping inherited money or property in your own name. It's not disloyal—it's simply good practice. You can generously share your property with your significant other while maintaining sole ownership of it.

MAKE A PLAN FOR YOUR
ENTIRE RETIREMENT PUZZLE

O UR CULTURE CALLS RETIREMENT *THE GOLDEN YEARS* and promises us that those years will be the ones in which we reap the rewards of our decades of hard work and the sacrifices we've made for our families. We are encouraged to look forward to the stage in life when we can kick back, enjoy leisure time, and live selfishly. It's a time for hobbies, travel, and the joy of grandkids without all the responsibilities.

Of course, the idea of a golden season of life is idealized. Retirement marks the end of our most productive years, when we contribute to society, create our nest egg, and form our legacy. The golden years mark the final phase of our life's journey. Thus, retirement involves a sense of loss and grief as well as relief.

Most of us anticipate retirement with mixed feelings. While we look forward to a season without the pressures of full-time work, we worry about the things we can only marginally control. For example, since we can't know how long we or our spouse will live, we can't know how long our savings have to last.

We might be able to guess at a magic number for savings but feel that number is beyond our reach. Since we can't know what health issues we will face, we are aware that purchasing long-term care insurance is a gamble—as is failing to purchase that insurance. If we have adult children who are still struggling to find their way, we don't know if we can count on them for help when we need it. And we don't know if we can be there until the end to care for our spouse or partner.

It's only natural to have retirement fears along with retirement hopes. The best way to manage both is to access the best information available and make a plan to control the things that are within our power. The chapters in this section will help you do just that.

CHAPTER 11

THINK OF 90 RATHER THAN 80 AS AN
AVERAGE LIFESPAN

LIFE EXPECTANCY IS A STATISTICAL MEASURE OF how long any given person may live, based on the year of birth, current age, and other factors. Multiple variables influence life expectancy, including lifestyle and genetics. Behaviors that increase life expectancy include marrying, exercising regularly, eating a healthy diet, driving safely, owning a pet, flossing your teeth daily, and keeping stress levels down. Yet, nothing is more important than genetics as a determinate of how long someone lives.

According to the Centers for Disease Control and Prevention's National Center for Health Statistics, the life expectancy in the United States is just under 80 years. You can check the latest tables at http://www.cdc.gov/nchs/fastats/life-expectancy.htm.

Published life expectancy tables, however, are just a starting place to figuring out how many years *your* money will need to last. Don't be surprised if you live past 80 years. For example, in a marriage in which both individuals are both currently age 65, there is a 47% chance of at least one partner living to age 90.

Many developed countries have a life expectancy of 80 to 85 years, higher than the United States by as much as 6 years. Japan is usually the leader, with life expectancy above 85. In 2015, life expectancy in Japan was 87 years. That is getting mighty close 90. In contrast, a life expectancy in Afghanistan was just 50 years.

The oldest confirmed recorded age for any human is 122 years, achieved by Jeanne Calment from Arles, France. Her life is believed to be the maximum life span possible, because it is the maximum number of years any human is known to have lived.

According to a United Nations Report, the number of centenarians in developed countries is increasing at approximately 5.5% per year, which means the centenarian population doubles every 13 years, pushing it from some 455,000 in 2009 to 4.1 million in 2050. Japan is the country with the highest ratio of centenarians, with 347 for every 1 million inhabitants as of September 2010. Misao Okawa (born 1898) is the oldest living person in the world as I write.

Depending upon where you look, you'll find mixed signals regarding life expectancy. Look at mortality tables used for life insurance, and you'll think you have a better chance of dying young; look at mortality tables used to sell annuities, and you'll think you'll live forever. Given the discrepancies, it's understandable that more than half of Americans underestimate their life expectancy. The financial planning time horizons of these individuals are accordingly (and tragically) too short.

As recently as the World War II generation, "old" was regarded to be about 60, which is not the case today. If the *average* person today will live until 80, that means half will live beyond 80 and half will die before 80. You, of course, can't know which category you or your spouse is in. It's safest to plan for a life expectancy of 90.

Ideas for long-term planning include the following:

- Pay off your mortgage or home equity loan to reduce your cost of living.

- Delay filing for Social Security to get a higher benefit and overcome inflation.

- Fund an annuity to increase retirement cash flow until death.

- Retire later or work part-time to delay the need to live off savings.

If you choose to delay your retirement or work part-time, you won't be alone. A Retirement Confidence Survey, conducted by Matthew Greenwald & Associates, shows that almost half of older workers are on the job longer than they had planned to be for about three additional years. In 2014:

- 32% of the labor force was age 65 to 69

- 19% of the labor force was age 70 to 74

- 11% of the labor force was age 75 to 79

Most people continue to work to serve their wants rather than their needs. For example, over 50% of those working claim they work to stay active and/or because they enjoy working. Just 25% say they need to work to make ends meet.

For most of us, it's hard to imagine living until we are 90, but this is certainly possible. Given this, and the fact that medical advancements are helping us to enjoy good health longer, it might be time to rethink our expectations to retire at 65. After all, 25 years (from 65 to 90) give us a lot of free time—as well as a need to finance those years.

Only you can decide what's right for you, your finances, and your ideal lifestyle. Whatever you decide, think in terms of a life expectancy of 90 rather than 80.

CHAPTER 12

CLARIFY YOUR VALUES SURROUNDING OLD AGE

R ETIREMENT IS A UNIQUE SEASON IN LIFE. Most of us think of it as the reward at the end of a lifetime of hard work, saving, and sacrificing. The idea of living life on our own terms—living a little selfishly—is more than appealing.

Even so, many of us fail to define what it means to live on our own terms. We may religiously save for the future (with spreadsheets and financial plans) without creating a clear picture of what we want that future to look like, day-by-day and year-by-year. Quality of life for seniors involves financial health, but it also includes so much more. You are most likely to enjoy your retirement years to the fullest if you answer the questions found in this chapter. Discuss the answers with your life partner and take steps before age 65 to ensure the retirement life of your dreams.

How Important Is It to You to Contribute Your Skills and Abilities to Society?

We saw in the last chapter than many seniors continue to work in order to stay active or because they enjoy it. Others want nothing to do with their former work life. Some simply want to golf, read, or spend time in other leisure activities.

As you think about retirement, consider the skills and abilities you have built over a lifetime. Is it important for you to continue in some way to contribute these assets to the community? If so, is the ideal a part-time job, a volunteer activity, or something else? Would you enjoy mentoring young professionals or teaching a college class?

If you answer these questions before you retire, you'll be better prepared to step into the life you choose. For example, you might choose to earn a certification in order to be attractive to the part-time job market, or pursue a degree that gives you the credentials to teach at a college or community level. Examples include certification as a professional coach, a master gardener, or a fitness instructor.

HOW IMPORTANT IS CONTINUAL LEARNING TO YOU?

Research tells us that a challenged mind ages more slowly than a stagnant one. What will work for you? Are you content to read and do crossword puzzles? Do you need structured mental challenges? Do you learn best on your own or in a group setting?

Many colleges offer academic and cultural experiences to seniors—and are even actively attracting retirees to their communities. In fact, a recent Kiplinger article names 10 great college towns in which to retire: http://www.kiplinger.com/slideshow/retirement/T006-S002-great-college-towns-to-retire-to/index.html. Is mental stimulation important enough for you to consider moving to one of these towns?

If you live near a college now, Osher Lifelong Learning Institute offers the opportunity for anyone to take noncredit courses on college campuses. No tests, grades, or educational requirements create barriers. Participants choose to learn from each other, hear opposing ideas, and synthesize the expertise of the instructor, the wisdom of their fellow students, and their own opinions into new views. Seniors involved with Osher Lifelong Learning Institute reconnect with the joy of learning and the passion connected to it. They say it keeps them in the mainstream and provides them an occasion to get dressed up in the morning.

WHAT KIND OF INVOLVEMENT DO YOU WANT WITH KIDS, GRANDKIDS, AND OTHER EXTENDED FAMILY MEMBERS?

In some families, grandkids are the #1 priority and interest for retirees. If this is true for you, what adjustments will you make in order to enjoy your grandkids to the fullest?

Do you plan to move in order to be ideally located? Do you plan to provide childcare to working parents? Does your home match your extended family and your goals for holidays and sleepovers? Do you plan to fund a family vacation at the beach or ski resort each year?

WHAT DOES THE IDEAL HOME AND COMMUNITY LOOK LIKE FOR YOU?

Are you planning to age in the home in which you've raised your family? If so, what adjustments will you need to make to the house? Would you prefer a condominium or other rental in which you no longer need to worry about upkeep? Would you enjoy the snowbird lifestyle, with a winter and summer location? Would you like to live in a community of retirees? Would you prefer an active, athletic community, an intellectual one, or one that caters to advancing health concerns?

WHAT RECREATIONAL OPPORTUNITIES ARE IMPORTANT TO YOU?

Older Americans are embracing an ever-expanding variety of activities. Golf is still the top fitness activity for seniors, with fishing and hunting close behind. Seniors, however, are pushing boundaries, especially physically, as they continue to ski, climb mountains, raft down rapids, and participate in adventure travel. While camping is still popular as people age, many retirees are choosing expensive motor homes over tents. The desire to engage with nature and other adventurers is a growing trend with the retirement community.

The U.S. Census ranked an age-restricted Florida community, called The Villages, as the fastest-growing U.S. city for the second year in a row (during the 12 months ended July 2014). The Villages boast 39 golf courses, some of which are championship courses. Residents of The Villages play free golf as a feature of their residency in the community. The community also has a number of recreational centers, activities, and cultural offerings.

While a community like The Villages might not be ideal for you, consider your need to stay active as you seek your own ideal community. Look for walking trails, easy access to shopping, and convenient access to healthcare.

HOW WILL YOU MEET YOUR NEEDS FOR SOCIAL COMMUNITY?

After a lifetime of working with colleagues outside of the home, retirement can be an isolating experience. Begin building a post-retirement social network before you retire. The opportunities are endless. For example, you might join a book club, tennis club, or a group at your church. You might build relationships around interests such as golf, bridge, or artistic pursuits.

Groups allow you to stay active, deflect boredom, and exercise your creative and social skills. As you plan retirement, plan to become involved and join something. Become a member of a group that will make you proud and happy.

HOW WILL HEALTHCARE CONCERNS INFLUENCE YOUR RETIREMENT DECISIONS?

There is no escaping the fact that healthcare needs increase with age. If you have health challenges prior to retirement, you have some idea of the steps you need to take to retire comfortably. If not, you'll still require access to high-quality healthcare. Be sure to balance this necessity with the other desires you have for your retirement.

Carefully consider your answers to each of the questions in this chapter. Those answers will help you look at your whole retirement picture and make decisions leading to the life you will really enjoy.

CHAPTER 13

UNDERSTAND ISSUES SURROUNDING LONG-TERM CARE

F EWER THAN 10% OF SENIORS currently purchase long-term care insurance, even though chances are good they will need this type of care. Health insurance, Medicare, and Medicaid have predetermined limits for the amount or number of days covered for home care, skilled nursing, and assisted living. Long-term care insurance helps provide for the cost of such care beyond these limits. This doesn't automatically mean that purchasing long-term care insurance is the right decision for you.

Let's look at some of the facts regarding long-term care before exploring strategies to pay for it. The groups most likely to need long-term care insurance are middle class single women and widowed spouses. Wealthy people can generally afford to pay their own way, and the genuinely poor will have to count on the government safety net. People in the middle may need long-term care insurance because they can't afford to pay their own way and don't want to jeopardize their wealth.

Statistics show that women, especially, are likely to need long-term care. In fact, women are expected to require long-term care at nearly double the rate of men, primarily due to their extended longevity.

A widowed spouse of either gender may need long-term health insurance after using up assets caring for the deceased spouse prior to passing.

A 2014 study, published by the Association for Long-Term Care Insurance 2014 Sourcebook (www.aaltci.org), provides the following facts:

- 73% of women under age 65, and 72% over age 65, will need long-term care.
- 35% of men under age 65, and 55% over age 65, will need long-term care.
- 79 is the average age at which a woman files her first claim against a long-term care policy.
- When looking at all long-term claims (men and women) by type, 25% will need home care, 58% will need a nursing home, and 17% will need assisted living.

While these statistics about the need for long-term care are staggering, the statistics regarding the cost of care are even more so. Since there's a good chance that you and/or your significant other will need long-term care, you need to make a plan for paying for this care. You have three basic options: private finance, public finance, and long-term care insurance.

PRIVATE FINANCE

People who have enough resources to pay for long-term care (roughly $2 million or more) may choose to self-insure. To finance your long-term care privately, you'll want to have enough principal to generate the income needed to pay for the cost of care without eroding your principal. Obviously, you'll also need to have enough liquidity or cash flow to pay the bills as they come.

If your resources don't provide enough cash flow, you can combine this option with others. As you make your decision about private financing any long-term care needs, consider the implications for your heirs in the process. Even if you can afford to self-pay, you might want a long-term care insurance policy in order to protect assets for your heirs.

PUBLIC FINANCE

Options in this category include Medicare, Medicaid, and the Veterans Administration. Nearly everyone over 65 is eligible for Medicare, but most people think this insurance covers more than it actually does. For example, in 2015, Medicare covered 100 days in a skilled nursing facility—only if the stay was preceded by a three-day minimum hospitalization.

Medicaid is a public-private partnership for those who have little money. Medicaid benefits cover at least the same healthcare services that Medicare does, as well as some services that Medicare doesn't. Separate Medicaid-funded programs cover long-term care, including nursing home care and in-home personal care. In some states, a Medicaid program will pay some of the costs of assisted living. Recipients must meet strict eligibility rules. Achieving eligibility often requires a spend-down of assets. Penalties are assessed for transferring assets less than 60 months before application.

Veterans of wartime service, their spouses, and widows may be eligible for money toward long-term care (called VA Aid and Attendance). Recipients must meet strict eligibility rules, and, again, a spend-down of assets is often required. There is no penalty for transferring assets.

LONG-TERM CARE INSURANCE

This insurance product helps provide for the cost of long-term care beyond a predetermined period set by your health insurance, Medicare, or Medicaid. The insurance helps pay for home care, assisted living, adult daycare, respite care, hospice care, nursing home care, and care at Alzheimer's facilities. Eligibility for services is need-related rather than age-related.

The price of long-term care insurance keeps going up. At the time of this writing, for example, a 55-year-old couple can expect to spend about $3,275 in annual premiums for $164,000 of coverage for each. That cost is expected to grow by 3% a year, equal to the rate of long-term inflation.

CHAPTER 14

CREATE A STRATEGY TO PREPARE FOR LONG-TERM CARE NEEDS

ASSUMING YOU DESIRE long-term care insurance—and you can afford it—this chapter provides basic guidelines for the purchase of long-term care insurance.

When purchasing long-term care insurance, recognize that you are purchasing a contract between the insurance company and yourself to cover an unknown expense far into the future. It is difficult for you and the insurance company to judge the actual expense accurately.

There are two options to pay for long-term care insurance. The first option is an open-ended contract. This is a contract in which the promises made by the insurance company can change from time to time. The insurance company can raise or lower benefits as well as premiums.

The second option is a closed contract (a completed contract) in which no changes are possible without agreement of both parties. The closed contract is both preferable and hard to find.

The obvious problem with an open-ended contract is that the benefits will inevitably go down and the price will inevitably go up. As you compare providers for an open-ended contract, look for companies that have a history of level premiums.

Here are some options that might save you money.

Buy Long-Term Care Insurance Long Before the Need Arises

The ideal time to purchase long-term care insurance is in your 50s, because premiums rise with age. Expect to pay double or triple when you get into your 60s.

Also, applicants who apply for long-term care insurance in their 60s and 70s may be rejected due to health-related issues.

Choose a Mutual Insurance Company

Mutual insurance companies are owned by their policyholders. The purpose of these companies is to provide insurance for policyholders, not maximize profits; hence, you can expect lower insurance costs. By contrast, stock insurance companies are owned and controlled by shareholders. Shareholders want a return on their investment; hence, you can expect higher insurance costs.

Purchase a Long-Term Care Insurance Policy Designed for Married Couples

This type of policy can double the coverage you receive. For example, if both partners purchase a two-year plan, one spouse can use all four years if needed.

PURCHASE A HYBRID LONG-TERM CARE INSURANCE POLICY

A hybrid policy mixes long-term care insurance with life insurance. With a hybrid policy, you pay a lump sum or monthly payments. If you don't use the long-term care portion of the policy, your heirs will get the remaining death benefit when you die. Be careful, however, because this could be the most expensive option. You are giving up a large amount of cash or payments that could be invested productively elsewhere.

Another type of hybrid policy utilizes an annuity with a long-term care rider. In this option, you buy an annuity, but rather than taking withdrawals, you earmark the money for long-term care. If it turns out don't need long-term care before the annuity matures, you can elect to receive the money or let it go to your heirs.

CHAPTER 15

OVERCOME RETIREMENT FEARS:
MAKE A PLAN FOR THE WORST-CASE SCENARIO

W E ALL HAVE RETIREMENT FEARS. It's easy—but not productive—to leave those fears lurking vaguely in the back of our minds. The best time to address your retirement fears and make a plan for the worst-case scenario is now. If your retirement situation is not bright, your fears may be justified. If your fears are justified, you need to resolve the underlying problems without delay. Dealing with the fears head-on will go a long way toward helping you to enjoy your golden years fully.

The realities behind some of the most common retirement concerns aren't as dire as you might expect. Here is some encouraging information about the most common ones.

I WON'T HAVE ENOUGH MONEY

This fear looms especially large in the face of increases in the average life expectancy. The possibility of outliving your money is real. You worry that you can't save enough, cut enough expenses, or maintain your lifestyle.

It's hard to resist worrying that you won't have enough, especially when many experts cite $3 million as a retirement savings goal (this is the old $1 million adjusted for inflation).

This $3 million dollars savings goal seems unattainable for many. The good news is that most people won't need this much. Why? This figure doesn't account for any other income sources, such as Social Security, pensions, rental properties, inheritance, or part-time work.

You need to identify a magic retirement goal number that reflects what's actually going to happen in *your* life post-retirement and figure out how to make up the difference. The best way to figure out your magic number and other realistic estimates is to work with an expert.

Work with a CERTIFIED FINANCIAL PLANNER™ (CFP®) before retirement to complete a comprehensive financial plan, because that plan is the closest thing to a crystal ball. This professional will work with you to create a plan that includes pre- and post-retirement income cash flow, fixed-income planning, calculated expenses, reallocated investments, and more. The expert support and knowledge will help make your transition smoother.

I WON'T GET SOCIAL SECURITY

With talk of Social Security's uncertain future rampant in the media, many people anticipating retirement fear there will be no Social Security payments left for them. Fear-driven articles make for good media, but that doesn't mean all the dire predictions will come true. The worst-case scenario is a reduction in benefits.

The 2014 OASDI Trustees Report states that reserves are projected to peak around 2020 and to be depleted around 2033 if no changes are made to the tax or benefit provisions before then. Once the reserves are depleted, estimates indicate that the government will be able to pay 77% of scheduled benefits from tax receipts alone.

The Social Security Board of Trustees projects that changes equivalent to an immediate reduction in benefits of about 17.4%, an immediate increase in the combined payroll tax rate from 12.4% to 15.23%, or some combination of these changes, would be sufficient to allow full payment of the scheduled benefits for the next 75 years.

I'll Feel Empty and Invisible in Retirement

Given a lifetime of juggling your work routine and your personal life, chances are you haven't had much time for extra activities. To avoid falling into a slump and experiencing the empty-agenda feeling, consider taking some hobbies more seriously, joining a local group, spending more time with friends and family, or planning an extended trip.

Your retirement will be what you make it. Think seriously about what energizes you and creates meaning and a sense of fulfillment for you, and be proactive in building those things into your life.

Some corporate executives, business owners, and other professionals feel invisible or diminished as they transition to retirement. The Type A personality often needs to be the "answer guy/gal" or center of attention, or at least contributing, to feel validated. When others stop asking questions, seeking their opinions, or making them the center of attention, a feeling of loss and worthlessness can set in.

If you anticipate this kind of a problem, join an organization that helps others who can benefit from your expertise. One example is SCORE, Senior Core of Retired Executives. SCORE coaches help people with new ventures and business startups, as well as advise established businesses that are experiencing problems.

Retirement is a perfect opportunity to contribute your skills, share your lessons learned, and mentor others. If you don't want to mentor business people, you can mentor teenagers or women re-entering the workforce. You might also consider volunteering on a non-profit board, spearheading a fundraising project, or becoming a literacy coach. There are countless ways to contribute and get your sense of purpose back. The good news is that you can contribute on your own terms.

I'LL BE LOST AS I MAKE THE TRANSITION

The year you retire is a transitional year. Keep your perspective and realize that no transition comes without its bumps and missteps. These issues can all cause sadness. At times, the stress of change will weigh heavily upon you; the nature of your friendships will change; and your relationship with your spouse or partner may change too.

None of this is reason to hit the panic button. Over time, things will work themselves out, and new opportunities will emerge. Retirement is the perfect time to find and try out new things. Seek out groups with similar interests as yours. Maybe a book club, bridge group, travel club, or dinner theater group is in your future. In the end, retirement can be the best portion of your life. All transitions are tough. Transitions, however, do end.

I WON'T BE ABLE TO AFFORD HEALTHCARE

Declining health and the rising cost of care is a natural—and realistic—concern to those approaching retirement. While maintaining your health can be expensive, insurance should help cover some of the costs.

With the Affordable Care Act, Medicare beneficiaries will save an average of $4,200 over the next 10 years due to lower drug costs, free preventive services, and reduced medical costs. The Medicare Part B premiums and prescription drug costs also have been lowered. The Affordable Care Act also hopes to reduce fraud, waste, and abuse, ultimately saving seniors money. These changes may help reduce overall medical costs in retirement.

MY INVESTMENTS WILL LOSE THEIR VALUE

Investing always involves some risk, and the fear that investment losses will ruin all you've worked for is normal. Fortunately, you can do something to address this fear. Reduce your risks by adjusting your investments as you get nearer to retirement. In general, you can take bigger risks when you are young and have more time to recover any potential losses. As you approach retirement, it's generally a good idea to invest more conservatively.

The current thinking surrounding investing for retirement assumes that you will live for decades in retirement, and you will require a very large and growing asset pool to draw from. Remember that you will not need 100% of your money on the first day of retirement. So, yes, investing involves risk, but so does longevity.

At the end of the day, you need to invest for the long term, (more than five years) but have enough in short-term assets (cash plus a diversified bond portfolio to cover a period of less than five years) to meet your short-term needs. This will enable you to take less from the stock portion of your portfolio in bad times, preserving the assets invested in stock with the expectation those assets will grow when the market rebounds.

I'LL NEED LONG-TERM CARE AND BE UNABLE TO AFFORD IT

With adults living longer than ever, the possibility that you will need medical or rehabilitative care in your retirement years is real. Chapter 13 in this book gives an overview of the options you have for financing this kind of care.

Investigating your options and making a plan before retirement will help you be prepared if the need for long-term care arises. If you decide to purchase long-term care insurance, do so as soon as you can. If you purchase the insurance when you are in your 50s, the cost will be much lower than if you wait. Whatever your choice, be proactive.

It's only natural to have fears surrounding retirement. Retirement marks a huge change in lifestyle, and there is no way to predict how long you will live or what needs you will have. Even so, if you face your fears with courage, work with a CFP® professional, and make and execute a realistic plan, you can face the future with confidence.

CHAPTER 16

MAKE A PLAN FOR YOUR LOVED ONES
IN THE EVENT OF DEATH

I F LEFT UNATTENDED, YOUR MONEY IS AT RISK FROM the realities of life, old age, and ultimately death. Without some advance planning, your family may not be in a position to pick up where you left off. At minimum, your spouse or another family member should know how, when, and where to pay for essential things such as property taxes and utilities. Everyday life keeps moving, even in the face of death.

At the time of death, however, family members must contend with things that require a great deal of physical and emotional energy. You give them a gift when you make sure that managing affairs doesn't require more energy than it should. Since even the best verbal communication is not enough to guide your family members through the issues, I recommend you prepare a Letter of Instruction to your family.

A Letter of Instruction is a document above and beyond your Last Will and Testament. This document outlines your instructions and desires regarding your affairs at the time of death, and it addresses the handling of the affairs of your estate. The Letter points out where to find your financial records and provides information regarding your beneficiaries. It expresses what you would like to say to your family and friends. It may also include an appendix detailing funeral plans and persons you wish to be notified of your passing.

At the time of death, your family members will face many questions. If you give consideration to these questions prior to death, you will save your family from extra angst at the worst time. Emotionally drained family members don't make the best decisions, especially when asked to do so in a short period. Your careful planning can relieve your family members of extra burdens while protecting the assets you leave.

Here is a short list of questions that should be answered in your Letter of Instruction:

1. Affairs at the Time of Death
   - Would you like to donate your organs?
   - Would you like to be cremated?
   - If you would like to be cremated, what would you like done with your ashes?
   - What are your requests surrounding your own funeral or memorial?
   - What would you like your obituary to say?
   - Where would you like your obituary to be published?

2. Affairs of the Estate
   - Where is the original will?
   - What is the contact information for the attorney who created the will?

- How do family members access any safety deposit boxes or safes?
- What decisions would you like the entire family or a specific party to make?

3. Overview of Financial Records
   - What are the details of cash flow before and after death?
   - Where is the life insurance policy or policies?
   - Who is the contact person, and what is the information for other insurance policies?
   - Where are the past tax returns and current tax information?
   - Where are the records of investments and other assets of value?
   - Where are your past and current bank records?
   - Where are your retirement assets and records?
   - Where are details on any outstanding debt?
   - Where are your computer records and passwords?

4. Message to Family and Friends
   - Which people should family members notify of your death?
   - What words of wisdom and love would you like to leave?

5. Appendix
   - What are the beneficiary designations of Insurance, Retirement Plans, and Transfer or Payable on Death or joint name in the title? These asset or account titles will direct assets to the beneficiary

noted in the title regardless of the Last Will and Testament instructions.

This is a long list of questions to answer and information to organize. As you age and near retirement, the thought of death may seem overwhelming, and organizing this much information can seem an exercise in futility. Even so, stay calm. You don't have to complete everything in one sitting, but don't procrastinate, either. Work on this document one question at a time.

Before you know it, you will have finished a complete and accurate Letter of Instruction to your family. The only thing left will be to update it periodically. This document will be of great value to your loved ones (whether they follow it or not)!

CHAPTER 17

ENSURE TAXES WON'T EAT AWAY AT ALL YOUR HARD WORK

WITH JUST A BIT OF KNOWLEDGE, you can defer some tax, reduce or avoid other taxes, and ultimately pay the least amount of tax. You need to learn the government rules and regulations so you know the game well enough to win. Here is a basic approach to paying the least amount of ordinary income tax, capital gains tax, and inheritance tax.

MANAGE ORDINARY INCOME WISELY

The complex tax code reveals a variety of ways to reduce or possibly eliminate some federal income tax. The income tax due each year is a function of the following: the asset base you have (both taxable assets and tax deferred); your charitable giving; and the amount of expenditures required to maintain your standard of living over the same period.

According to the Tax Policy Center, 43.3% of American households paid no federal income tax in 2013, a percentage that sounds alarming! Of course, income tax is only one of many taxes we pay each year. While federal income tax is generally the largest portion of the overall taxes paid annually, dozens of other taxes come into play as well. These include property, sales, gas, liquor, Social Security, state, and local taxes. We also pay taxes in the form of licensing and permit fees.

When you derive some of your income from Social Security, you'll discover that some benefits are tax-free and some are partially taxable, depending on your income level. Theoretically, Social Security distributions should be entirely tax free—because you have already paid tax on what you have contributed to Social Security. In the early years of an individual collecting Social Security, however, the taxable portion of distributions is actually taxed twice by the same taxing authority, the federal government.

How can a taxpayer reduce federal income tax liability? The answer depends on the source of the income as well as the deductions and credits you can apply. Nothing is simple, so be sure to consult a qualified professional. Here are some general tips.

1. Consider Investing in Municipal Bonds
   Because they provide tax-free interest, many wealthy investors allocate a good portion of their portfolio to municipal bonds. There is, however, a trade-off involved. With municipal bonds, you get a lower pre-tax return than you would on taxable bonds; however, the after-tax return can be greater if it lowers your income tax bracket.

2. Take Full Advantage of Credits and Deductions
   If you're self-employed, you can deduct some or all of your health insurance premiums outside the standard deduction without itemizing. If you

itemize, you can deduct qualified medical expenses that exceed 10% of adjusted gross income.

If you have to make expensive capital improvements to a home to accommodate an illness or injury, your deductions can result in significant tax savings. (The deduction is 7.5% for taxpayers over the age of 65).

The ultra-wealthy can reduce federal income taxes by establishing certain trusts that will pay the income tax and pass the assets on to future generations. Wealthy business owners who have a significant gross income may reduce their taxable income to nearly nothing by deducting business expenses. Wealthy individuals may also choose to give away assets to family members, thereby reducing the size of their estate. They may also give to charity in an effort to reduce their federal income tax.

If you aren't ultra-wealthy, be sure to research deductions and credits applicable to you. These provisions can drastically reduce federal income taxes.

UNDERSTAND THE RULES AROUND CAPITAL GAINS TAX AND TIMING

A capital gain occurs when you sell something for more than you spent to acquire it. This rule applies to both investments and personal property. For example, if you buy a classic car for $40,000 and sell it for $50,000 a week later, you have a

$10,000 capital gain. The tax implications are the same as when you buy a stock for $10,000 and sell it for $20,000. Every taxpayer needs to understand a few basic facts about capital gains taxes.

If you sell something for more than your *basis* in the item, then the difference is a capital gain, and you'll need to report that gain on your taxes. Your basis is usually what you paid for the item. It includes the price of the item, plus any other costs you paid to acquire it, including sales taxes, excise taxes, other taxes and fees, shipping related costs, and any improvements that increased the value.

Of course, things don't always go up in value. They also go down. If you sell something for less than its basis, you have a capital loss. You can use capital losses from investments (not personal property) to offset capital gains. For example, if you have $30,000 in long-term gains from the sale of one stock, but $20,000 in long-term losses from the sale of another, then you are only required to pay tax on $10,000 worth of long-term capital gains.

If your capital losses exceed capital gains, you may be able to use the loss to offset up to $3,000 of ordinary income. If you have more than $3,000 in capital losses, you can carry the excess forward to future years to offset income in those years. There is no ceiling on how much capital loss a taxpayer can carry forward.

The best thing about the capital gains tax is that you get to decide when you pay it. With individual stocks, capital gains tax is triggered only when you sell, so if you hold onto your shares for the long run, you'll go for years or decades without owing any tax. Unfortunately, that's not the case for mutual funds, as you can owe tax on capital gains distributions even if you don't sell the shares.

The only way to avoid capital gains tax completely is to die. When you die, your assets get a *step-up* in basis. This effectively voids capital gains as of the date of your death. Heirs get assets without capital gains tax liability, unless there is growth between the date of death and the time of actual receipt of the asset or security.

Income from long-term capital gains is not taxed as federal income, but at a lower capital gains rate. That rate can actually be zero for those in the 10% or 15% tax brackets. For example, in 2015, a married couple with adjusted gross income below $74,900, heads of household below $50,200, and single taxpayers below $37,450 might pay no tax on net capital gains.

Even if you make more than the maximum amount for the 10% or 15% filing status, you may be able to take advantage of the zero capital gain rate. This is because the cutoff amounts for income are based upon taxable income, not the larger adjusted gross income amount. So calculate your taxable income first to estimate capital gains tax due prior to making a sale.

STRUCTURE YOUR ASSETS TO BE INHERITANCE FRIENDLY

Inheritance tax rates are determined by the relationship of the beneficiary to the decedent and the type of property involved.

The federal inheritance tax exemption rises to $5.43 million per person in 2015. A married couple gets $10.86 million of federal inheritance tax free transfer of assets at the time of death. If your estate exceeds this amount, you might consider some of the following.

1. Give Away Some of the Money
   It may seem counterintuitive, but sometimes it makes sense to give a portion of your inheritance to others. You will help those in need, reduce the size of your estate, and avoid future federal inheritance tax. You could also potentially offset the taxable income on your inheritance with the tax deduction you receive for donating to a qualified charitable organization.

2. Give Annual Gifts to Your Beneficiaries While You're Still Living
   In 2015, you could give $14,000 per person or $28,000 per couple without being subject to gift taxes. Gifting not only provides an immediate benefit to your loved ones, it reduces the size of your estate.

3. Consider an Alternate Valuation Date
   Typically, the basis of property in a decedent's estate is the fair market value of the property on the date of death. In some cases, however, the executor might choose the alternate valuation date, which is six months after the date of death. The top federal estate tax rate is 40%. This is a good reason to do the math.

While states vary in their legislation regarding inheritance tax exemptions, certain principles are common to all.

The surviving spouse usually pays no state inheritance tax. Parents or children of the decedent pay the least percentage of inheritance tax. For example, beneficiaries who are either a parent or a child of a decedent pay 4.5%, and siblings pay 12% Pennsylvania Inheritance Tax. In Pennsylvania, family heirs can also claim a $3,500 tax exemption from inheritance tax.

If you are looking to move family assets into future generations, research your state regulations. For example, Pennsylvania allows inheritance tax exemptions for certain kinds of property. Farmland is exempt from inheritance tax, as long as the land is inherited by family members and continues to be used for agriculture for seven years (effective for deaths as of July 2, 2012). Small family-owned businesses with fewer than 50 employees and assets valued at less than $5 million are also exempt from inheritance tax, if they have been in existence at least five years, are inherited by family members, and stay in operation for another seven years, (effective July 9, 2013).

You can't escape taxes, but with some knowledge, you can defer some tax, reduce or avoid other taxes, and ultimately pay the least amount of tax.

CHAPTER 18

PLAN FOR INFLATION

L OW INFLATION OCCURS WHEN PRICES RISE 3% a year or less. According to the U.S. Federal Reserve, when prices rise 2% or less, it's beneficial to economic growth. This is because inflation at this low level sets expectations that prices will continue to rise. As a result, demand increases as consumers decide to buy now before prices rise in the future. By increasing demand, low inflation drives economic expansion.

An above-average level of inflation occurs when price levels rise between 3% and 10% a year. This level is bad for the economy because it increases economic growth too fast. People buy more just to avoid tomorrow's higher prices. This drives demand even further, and suppliers can't keep up—and wages don't keep pace either. As a result, common goods and services are priced out of the reach of most people.

High inflation occurs when price levels rise to 10% or higher. High inflation wrecks an economy. Money loses value so fast that income can't keep up with costs and prices. Foreign investors avoid the country, depriving it of needed capital. The economy becomes unstable, and government leaders lose credibility. High inflation must be avoided at all costs.

Deflation, the opposite of inflation, occurs when prices fall. Deflation occurs when an asset bubble bursts. This is what happened to Internet stocks in 2000 and housing in 2006. In fact, the Federal Reserve was worried about over-all deflation during these recessions. Deflation can turn a recession into a depression.

The Federal Reserve targets a 2% inflation rate for the good of the economy. To keep inflation under control, the government uses monetary policy. The Federal Reserve's most effective method of controlling inflation is through the contraction of monetary policy (making less money available).

One way the Feds change monetary policy is by raising the target for the Federal funds rate (aka the overnight bank lending rate). This increases the rate that banks charge each other to borrow funds to meet the reserve requirement for banks. This reserve requirement is the amount the Federal Reserve requires banks to have on deposit each night when they close their books. This requirement ensures banks will have enough cash to cover operating expenses if any of the loans default.

This action by the feds increases interest rates because the banks pass the increased reserve costs to their customers. It helps reduce spending because people feel they have less to spend. Less spending means people keep their money and save it. Reduced spending helps slow down the economy and, in turn, the rate of inflation.

A second contractionary monetary policy tool the Federal Reserve uses to combat inflation is to increase the amount banks must keep in reserve (bank reserve requirement). This contracts money available because banks charge higher interest rates on their loans to compensate for the higher amount they must keep in reserve. As a result, businesses borrow less, don't expand as much, and hire fewer workers, decreasing demand.

The government can also adjust the money supply by enacting policies that encourage the increase or reduction of the money supply. For example, the Federal Reserve buys government bonds in the open market when they want to increase monetary supply, making more money available in the marketplace. When the government desires less money in the marketplace, they sell government bonds, decreasing the amount of money available to spend.

Low Inflation, Which We Currently Have, Helps Retirees

Many retirees complain about the amount of income from their retirement and bank savings. As I write this, a 10-year Treasury bill pays less than 3% interest. The average stock in the S&P 500 yields less than 2%. If you want the safety of a bank CD, you get less than 1% interest.

If you've been lucky enough to put together $1 million, and you are a serious conservative investor, you receive just $1,250 monthly on a return of 1.5%. After tax, you will have even less to spend and pay bills. This is the reason some say the new million (magic number for retirement savings) is $3 million.

The main reason for the current paltry interest rates is low inflation. Yes, prices still tick up a little bit here and there, but costs for many items have gone down. However, the cost of healthcare will continue to go up because of increased demand; the baby boomer generation is settling into its retirement years.

Retirees should be happy with low inflation because it benefits them more than any other group. Retirees, particularly those on a fixed income, benefit from low inflation. A pension, if you are lucky enough to have one, is likely not indexed to inflation.

HIGHER INFLATION IS COMING; TAKE STEPS TO PROTECT YOURSELF

We are currently in the early stages of what is being called the Federal Reserve's *great unwind*. This means that the government is reducing the amount of bonds and assets it is purchasing to keep interest rates low. With the ease in government spending comes the potential threat of rising inflation.

Even low inflation is a concern for retirees. While a 2.5% rate of inflation might not appear to be high, it would double the cost of consumer goods every 28 years. This could cause some difficulty for retired persons living on a fixed income.

If there is a significant increase in the minimum wage, wage/price inflation may be especially difficult to contain, as higher wages lead to higher prices, which then necessitate even higher wages to keep up. Retirees should be concerned. Inflation could hurt people living on a fixed income. Here are steps you can take to overcome the effects of inflation.

1. Forgo an Early Retirement
   If your retirement income and assets are not sufficient to provide a sizable cushion in the event of
   economic downturns and other emergencies, keep
   working for a while. Remember: it is better to
   work longer at a job that pays well even if you
   don't like it. Finding a lower paying job at an ad-
   vanced age can be even more painful.

2. Delay Social Security Income Distributions
   If you have not started drawing Social Security
   payments, wait until age 70. You will receive an
   eight percent annual increase each year you wait.
   Waiting until 70 to collect will result in 124% of
   normal retirement benefits.

3. Consider Investing in Inflation-Protected Securities
   Treasury Inflation Protected Securities (TIPS) and,
   to lesser extent, inflation protected savings bonds
   (I-Bonds) can both provide protection against in-
   flation. You can invest in TIPS directly from the
   U.S. Treasury or through a mutual fund. Purchase
   I-Bonds directly from the U.S. Treasury, $10,000
   maximum per-person annually.

4. Consider Bank Loan Funds, also Known as Float-
   ing Rate Bonds or Senior Secured Notes
   The rate of dividend the owner collects on these
   investments is tied to the London Interbank Of-
   fered Rate, (LIBOR index); the rate resets every 90
   days. When interest rates rise, the dividend rate
   for the security rises within 90 days too. These
   funds are asset-backed. While they are backed by

collateral, they are risky, and are best purchased through mutual funds. A mutual fund will provide the needed protective diversification.

5. Consider Purchasing Commodities
   While volatile, commodities values will rise with the demand associated with rising prices. Unless you are an expert commodities trader, a quality mutual fund is your best bet here, too.

6. Consider an Annuity with an Inflation Rider
   This kind of annuity can protect against inflation, but it does come with negative aspects. For example, in order to receive inflation protection under an annuity payment plan, you'll need to annuitize your annuity investment first. Once the annuity is annuitized, the principle is gone forever. Plus, the inflation protection of the annuity income stream will cost about one-quarter of your income. For example, if you can obtain an income of $1,000 monthly, the same annuity with inflation protection will pay out $750. Inflation protection can be very expensive.

The very best solution for dealing with the effects of inflation is to learn to live with it and balance risk. Stocks and bonds are most risky in the short term, so own stocks and bonds for the long term. Start early and hold your stocks and bonds long term. At the end of the day, because of longevity, learning to live with risk is a better bet than living without risk. Learning to live with risk means you must consider investments that do not come with a guarantee.

Because of their low return rates, guaranteed investments are good for short-term needs to the detriment of long-term needs. To build wealth, shift your focus from short-term returns to longer investment horizons where equity returns are likely to outpace inflation. Don't fall into the trap of underestimating your lifespan and focusing entirely on guaranteed low returns. Remember that 90 is the new 80, and consider stocks for the long term.

SECTION 4

MAKE PEACE WITH YOUR OWN MISTAKES

W E THINK OF MONEY in terms of numbers, manifested objectively in dollars and cents. We use money in certain situations, such as grocery shopping or banking. The transactions we make at such locations are logical, even if sometimes complex.

For much of life, we push thoughts of money aside. For example, when we are eating our groceries, the money is mostly out-of-mind, in our wallets or virtual accounts, waiting until we need it again. If we believe we have made good financial decisions, we expect or hope the money is quietly growing according to its logical rules. In the meantime, we carry on with our lives.

We may act as if money is its own separate category, and an objective one at that, but this is far from true. Money is woven intricately into everything in us and around us, including our personalities and every relationship.

For example, if we have an over-confident ego, we may insist on controlling every aspect of our lives, even those aspects in which we have no qualifications—and no time to acquire them. We may choose to make all our money decisions without help—to our own detriment. We just won't trust anyone else.

On the other hand, if we have an under-confident ego, we may inadvertently become dependent on another family member to take care of our finances, even if we would do a better job. We may abdicate decisions we should be making and limit our freedom in the process.

When it comes to relationships, shame and guilt enter into financial affairs as powerfully as they do in emotional affairs. We often make financial decisions based on deeply held values we learn from our first family, including what it means to love and support family members, including adult kids and dysfunctional cousins.

The essays in this section all address some aspect of money and mistakes. Some of the essays are concerned with financial management practices—the more logical side of money. Others make a case for which advisors you should trust and which ones you should not. Still other essays are concerned with the way money mixes with emotions of guilt and shame.

Chances are you'll recognize yourself in some of the mis-perceptions and mistakes described in this chapter, so no worries about that. While it's never easy to face a mistake, the best way forward is to learn from the mistake and move on. The essays in this section will help you do just that.

CHAPTER 19

CHECK YOUR EGO—AND THE NEED TO CONTROL EVERYTHING—AT THE DOOR

I F YOU ARE SMART AND KNOW IT, your own ego can be a formidable enemy. Individuals who know they are smart often insist on controlling all investment decisions even when they have neither the necessary expertise nor the time to acquire and maintain that expertise. While you may be successful in controlling most areas of your life, no one has the ability to control it all. Because of the complications involved, it is risky to endeavor to control all aspects of your own wealth. An inflated ego can leave an investment portfolio devastated. A great investment experience starts by checking your ego at the door.

Here are profiles of egos that can destroy your life savings. See if you recognize yourself or someone you know in one of the following scenarios.

THE OVER-CONFIDENT EGO
There is a fine line between confidence and over-confidence. Confidence is a healthy attribute. It makes us feel good about ourselves and take reasonable risks. Over-confidence is part

of a belief system that convinces you that you are smarter than everyone else. Believing this doesn't make it true.

Over-confidence causes investors to seek proof that confirms their own views only. They develop blind spots to contradicting evidence. For example, over-confident investors might think diversification is only for others; they may ignore established investment wisdom and concentrate assets because they believe they can foresee the future and successfully time the market.

You may have studied and worked hard, and you may have a sense that you have the pulse of the market. Do not fool yourself. Any large investment you make based upon unwise and unrealistic expectations will cause you to work longer and harder well into the future.

Study and hard work in investing does not necessarily translate into higher returns. Does your confidence lead you to believe you know something the market doesn't already know? Do you believe you have unique knowledge of a stock, a bond, an exchange-traded fund (ETF), or a mutual fund manager that others just don't know? If so, chances are you are kidding yourself.

THE LIVING LIKE A KING TODAY EGO

An out-of-control ego will encourage you to live beyond your means, spend when you should be saving, and focus on achieving unrealistically high investment returns. If you have a five-figure salary, you'll be tempted to live as if you have a six-figure salary. If you have a six-figure salary, you'll be tempted to live as if you have a seven-figure salary. In either case, you are courting disaster when you live above your means, expecting a windfall.

The smart, humble, and realistic thing to do is straight-forward—pay yourself first. Save at least 10 to 20% of your annual income. There will come a time when either you want to retire or are forced to retire. Don't cheat your future self because you have a big ego and want to overspend today.

Keep this reality in mind: In the early years of accumulating wealth, the amount you save is much more important than your investment returns. Investment returns matter more after you have built up a substantial portfolio. While it's never wise to live above your means, it's especially unwise in your younger years.

THE UNDERESTIMATING RISK EGO

Having lived through the Great Recession (or learning from those who did) is one of the best lessons about risk you can experience in your lifetime. In the heart of the 2007-2009 Great Recession, active and index stock investors realized a 33% or 50% decline, respectively. If you had money in stocks, you know what this can look and feel like. This knowledge should now be your gauge for risk.

Because the Great Recession started out as a credit crisis, bonds and bond fund values declined as well as stocks. Only U.S. Treasury securities held up during this period. If you had an inflated ego prior to the Great Recession, you took too much risk and probably had too much investment in stock.

You weren't alone in this mistake. Make sure, however, that you learn from the experience. Many investors refuse to learn, saying, "It can't happen again." Remember: The worst risk is the downfall you believe can never happen.

Here is a good rule of thumb: Expect that the stock portion of your portfolio might decline as much as 50% in any given year. With a 50% stock portfolio, assuming the other 50% is stable, you should expect to lose 25% in one year. Keep a stable portion available, so you do not have to use deflated investment money to pay bills.

THE GAMBLER EGO

If you like to go to a casino, you know that the wise approach is to take a set amount—an amount you are comfortable losing. The first rule with investing, however, is not to get comfortable losing money at all, but to take a conservative approach and diversify. Don't confuse gambling with investing. In other words, don't gamble with investments.

Many folks do exactly this—gamble with their retirement—without realizing it. The difference between gambling and investing is that gambling hinges on hope and a limited time. People hope to parlay their gambling into something, but they expect to lose. Gambling happens over a short period, less than 24 hours. Investing happens over a much longer period (decades), and the expectation and need is to gain, not lose.

Here are examples of how people gamble with investments. Avoid everything on this list:

- Buying individual stocks or bonds that currently pay high dividends
- Buying sector funds

- Buying individual asset classes
- Buying individual commodities
- Picking last year's winning mutual fund manager
- Shorting stocks
- Buying inverse funds
- Timing the market

Instead, invest by capturing the return of the market. You can do this through low-cost diversified mutual funds, but there are tax implications with this strategy. The better option for after-tax accounts is a well-diversified individual stock and bond portfolio. Try to replicate the market with your portfolio here too. A hybrid portfolio may also work—a well-diversified individual stock portfolio with bond mutual funds.

THE EGGS IN ONE BASKET EGO

If you could place a bet with an amount equivalent to the value of your house or retirement portfolio on the very best horse at the races, and win, you would make the most possible money. On the other hand, you could lose everything. Betting on that one very best horse is equivalent to a concentrated investment portfolio, something I see all the time.

For example, I see many corporate executives with too much of their assets in their own company's stock. Others believe that buying household names such as Apple, Microsoft, Intel, and Verizon equals a diversified portfolio. Even investing in a dozen different stocks doesn't add up to a well-diversified portfolio, the kind you need to mitigate risk.

A healthy portfolio of diversity can instantly be obtained with good mutual funds. Due to the nature of how mutual funds are taxed, they work best for you in a retirement savings plan. Investment management fees do affect your returns; however, the risk-adjusted return is the bigger consideration.

What can you do to combat your ego and need to control? The first step is becoming aware. Learn to observe your ego and recognize the signs that it is flaring up. Otherwise, you will not be able to contain your ego before it lands you in trouble. If or when you see yourself in any of the six wake-up calls listed below, take action, because your ego is in control and putting your financial situation in danger. They include the following:

- You are a fighter.
- You are impatient.
- You are judgmental.
- You are a sore loser.
- You are self-centered.
- You are smarter than most everyone around you.

If you see your ego flaring up through one of the wake-up calls above, stop and take a break. Rather than following your controlling ego, redirect, and focus on your desired character to make better decisions based upon love and compassion.

Remember, the worst ego-related shortcoming is to fail to learn from your prior mistakes. Pay attention for any of the wake-up calls above, and lose the ego before you make another mistake with your investments.

CHAPTER 20

GIVE YOURSELF PERMISSION
TO TRUST A FIDUCIARY

D EALING WITH YOUR DRIVE TO CONTROL everything in your life is tough, but failing to deal with this urge in financial matters can bring devastating results. For the benefit of your family and your future, find the courage to trust the appropriate professional. In this case, the appropriate professional is a fiduciary, who is both an expert in the financial arena and obligated to keep your best interests as top priority. When you give yourself permission to trust a fiduciary rather than trying to manage all aspects of money on your own, you will get better results as well as greater peace of mind.

Of course, learning to trust others to manage your own money is difficult—because money is precious, mistakes are costly, and swindlers exist. It's hard to let go and trust. On the other hand, your own lack of objectivity and ego-related mistakes could be bigger enemies than the external ones you perceive. In order to make good financial decisions, you must be objective—not influenced by personal feelings in considering facts.

Let's dig into the definition of a legal fiduciary and the designations of CERTIFIED FINANCIAL PLANNER™ (CFP®) and Registered Investment Adviser (RIA). I'll make the case that you can and should trust the CFP®s and RIAs, even though they are not legal fiduciaries. Because I am a CFP® myself, you may think I'm biased. Even so, I hope you will hear me out. In case you still prefer not to work with a fiduciary, I'll end this chapter with advice on how to trust someone who is not a fiduciary.

WHAT IS A FIDUCIARY?

A fiduciary is an individual or other entity (such as corporate fiduciary, which is often the trust department of a local bank) who has a legal and ethical relationship of trust between himself or herself and one or more other parties. Typically, a fiduciary prudently takes care of money for another individual. Other fiduciaries include mutual fund companies, managers of pension plans and endowments, and more.

From a legal standpoint, a fiduciary relationship typically occurs when a person (the principal) is in a diminished capacity or a vulnerable state and is willing to pay for the services of the fiduciary. The vulnerable person assumes the other party will act in good faith. In this arrangement, the fiduciary is legally required to act at all times for the sole benefit and interest of the principal.

A fiduciary duty is the highest standard of care. A fiduciary is expected to be acutely loyal to the principal. There must be no actual conflict of interest between fiduciary and principal, and the fiduciary is obligated to expose all potential conflicts of interest. Moreover, the principal must sanction the method by which the fiduciary is paid for services rendered.

SHOULD YOU TRUST A CFP® EVEN THOUGH THE PERSON IS NOT LEGALLY A FIDUCIARY?

The answer to this question is, yes!

The CFP® designation is a professional certification mark for financial planners. To be a CFP®, an individual must meet education, examination, experience, and ethical requirements. While the CFP® practitioner is not technically a legal fiduciary, the CFP® Board Code of Ethics and Professional Responsibility are binding for a CFP® in practice. The exact code is listed below. As you can see by the seven principles of this code, the obligations of the CFP® go beyond the tenants of a fiduciary.

Principle 1 – Integrity
Provide Professional Services with Integrity

Integrity demands honesty and candor which must not be subordinated to personal gain and advantage. Certificants are placed in positions of trust by clients, and the ultimate source of that trust is the certificant's personal integrity. Allowance can be made for innocent error and legitimate differences of opinion, but integrity cannot co-exist with deceit or subordination of one's principles.

Principle 2 – Objectivity
Provide Professional Services Objectively

Objectivity requires intellectual honesty and impartiality. Regardless of the particular service rendered or the capacity in which a certificant functions, certificants should protect the integrity of their work, maintain objectivity, and avoid subordination of their judgment.

Principle 3 – Competence
Maintain the Knowledge and Skill Necessary to Provide Professional Services Competently

Competence means attaining and maintaining an adequate level of knowledge and skill, and application of that knowledge and skill in providing services to clients. Competence also includes the wisdom to recognize the limitations of that knowledge and when consultation with other professionals is appropriate or referral to other professionals necessary. Certificants make a continuing commitment to learning and professional improvement.

Principle 4 – Fairness
Be Fair and Reasonable in All Professional Relationships

Disclose conflicts of interest. Fairness requires impartiality, intellectual honesty, and disclosure of material conflicts of interest. It involves a subordination of one's own feelings, prejudices and desires so as to achieve a proper balance of conflicting interests. Fairness is treating others in the same fashion that you would want to be treated.

Principle 5 – Confidentiality
Protect the Confidentiality of All Client Information

Confidentiality means ensuring that information is accessible only to those authorized to have access. A relationship of trust and confidence with the client can only be built upon the understanding that the client's information will remain confidential.

Principle 6 – Professionalism
Act in a Manner That Demonstrates Exemplary Professional Conduct

Professionalism requires behaving with dignity and courtesy to clients, fellow professionals, and others in business-related activities. Certificants cooperate with fellow certificants to enhance and maintain the profession's public image and improve the quality of services.

Principle 7 – Diligence
Provide Professional Services Diligently

Diligence is the provision of services in a reasonably prompt and thorough manner, including the proper planning for, and supervision of, the rendering of professional services.

SHOULD YOU TRUST A RIA EVEN THOUGH THE PERSON IS NOT LEGALLY A FIDUCIARY?

The answer to this question is also, yes!

An RIA is an investment adviser (IA) registered with the Securities and Exchange Commission (SEC) or a state's securities agency. An IA is defined by the SEC as an individual or a firm that is in the business of giving advice about securities. Investment advisers receive compensation for giving advice on investing in various securities and for managing portfolios of securities. IAs do not receive commissions from selling products.

The Fiduciary Standard of Care requires that a financial adviser act solely in the client's best interest when offering personalized financial advice. An IA must adhere to a fiduciary standard of care laid out in the U.S. Investment Advisers Act of 1940. This standard requires IAs to act and serve a client's best interests with the intent to eliminate conflicts of interest which might incline an IA (consciously or unconsciously) to render advice which are not in the best interest of the IA's clients.

WHAT IF YOU PREFER TO WORK WITH NON-FIDUCIARIES?

Some people are uncomfortable dealing with fiduciaries because they feel the sense of security that comes with this relationship is false. If this describes you, consider the following guidelines, as well as your gut feeling. When you listen to your gut feeling, it will tell you whether you are dealing with someone with integrity, good intent, and competence who will help you achieve your goals. When focused, your gut feeling will help you find the way.

> ### Listen and Look for Clues That Indicate You Are Dealing with Someone with Integrity
>
> Ask yourself, does this person walk the talk? Does he or she follow through on promises? Make commitments he or she can't keep? Promise things and not deliver?

Listen and Look for Good Intent

Good intent or motive becomes apparent with careful observation. Ask yourself what motivates this person. Is he or she motivated by a sense of mission—or just by your money? Is the person here to help you or help himself?

Look for Competence

Are this person's capabilities relevant to your needs? Does he or she have the ability to solve your problems? Does the person possess the abilities to deliver what is most important to you? Can you find value in the deliverables?

Look for a Results-Oriented Perspective

At the end of the day, you want results. You want to achieve goals. Ask yourself if the person you are speaking with is an enterprising person. Will he or she take ownership in order to achieve the desired results for you? Ask for and get evidence of a record of accomplishment for delivering your desired outcome.

The ultimate concern, whether you are working with a fiduciary or not, is that the person cares about you and will act in your best interest. In order to manage your investments wisely, *you do need* the expertise and objectivity of a professional.

CHAPTER 21

WATCH OUT FOR UNQUALIFIED ADVISORS

H AVE YOU EVER FOLLOWED FRAUDULENT investment advice? Before you shout, "No!" think carefully. Chances are you've at least listened to unqualified advice, which can be unwittingly fraudulent advice.

The fact is, all of us hear unqualified investment advice on a regular basis. It might come from a sibling, cousin, friend, neighbor, bank teller, or an unregistered insurance salesperson. Investment advice is considered fraudulent when an untrained and unregistered person gives a recommendation or guidance that attempts to educate, inform, or guide an investor regarding a particular investment product or series of products. This happens every day, and most often, the advisor has only the best of intentions.

All of us are inundated on a daily basis with tips and financial advice that can cost us lots of money. Extending beyond commercial advertising, we get unqualified advice from friends, family, television personalities, media pundits, and financial gurus. Unfortunately, the advice is often bad or too late to do us any good. We're told to invest in hot trends, often causing bubbles that end poorly. In such situations, by the time we invest, the price has gone up and the bubble is about to burst.

Sometimes the unqualified advice comes from someone who thinks he or she has information and is looking to help you cash in. Perhaps the insider is the brother-in-law of your oldest sibling who works at Future Social Media Corporation. This person gives your sibling a tip about a revolutionary new service that Future Social Media Corporation is about to launch. According to the insider, "This new service will sell like hot cakes and just can't miss." In response, you, your sibling, and half your family buy Future Social Media Corporation's stock. The new service bombs and you all lose big.

Advice from misguided financial professionals can also be iffy, especially when they work on a commission basis. Commission-based financial advisors have an inherent conflict of interest between their own and their clients' interests. I'm not suggesting that commission-based financial advisors are bad people, only that they naturally feel pressure to pay their bills.

Commission-based financial advisors are often pressed to or given incentives to push specific products. These products may or may not be in their clients' best interests. The financial incentives can influence the advice these advisors give and the facts they disclose.

For example, advisors are paid high commissions on the sales of variable annuities. When a misguided financial advisor urges a client to buy a variable annuity, even though it may not be the best possible investment for the client, the conflict of interest has raised its ugly head. The client, who trusts the knowledge of the advisor, loses.

If you have made any of the mistakes described so far in this chapter, forgive yourself and move forward. Learn from your mistakes and trust only qualified advisors from now on. A good beginning is to understand the distinctions behind certifications and designations in the financial field.

Dozens of different financial advisor designations exist. The requirements for these designations differ greatly. Some take years of education, experience, and continuing education, while others can be obtained in a three-hour course. You need to know the meaning behind each designation.

The Investment Advisers Act of 1940 is a federal law created to protect you by regulating the actions of providing investment advice for compensation. The Act defines an "investment adviser" as anyone who, for compensation, engages in the business of advising others about the value of securities or the advisability of investing in, purchasing, or selling securities. It's against the law for an unqualified advisor to provide advice in these matters. The following guidelines will clarify who is legally qualified and who is not.

INVESTMENT ADVISORS AND STOCKBROKERS

Within the financial industry, some designations are earned, and some come merely by virtue of registering to do business in a certain category. The experience of the provider, the payment structure, and the ethical standards differ widely.

CERTIFIED FINANCIAL PLANNER™ (CFP)®

A CFP® is the most respected financial advisor designation. An individual with this designation has earned it by rigorous training and ethical commitment. The basic requirements for a CFP® include at least 3 years of experience in the financial services industry and either a bachelor's degree or 5 years of financial planning experience. To be certified, an applicant must pass a 6-hour exam that covers financial planning, taxes, insurance, estate planning, and retirement. To maintain certification, the individual must demonstrate high ethical conduct and complete 30 hours of continuing education every two years. A CFP® is obligated to place the client's interest over his or her own.

A CFP® is paid to offer financial advice, not to sell products. You typically pay a percentage of your assets for the service. A CFP® is qualified to help you with investments, insurance, estate planning, corporate benefits, retirement, and income tax planning. A CFP® also knows his or her limits and recommends other experts such as lawyers, accountants, and insurance professionals as appropriate.

Registered Representative (a.k.a. Stockbroker)

A Registered Representative can mean a number of things, depending upon how the individual or firm registers to do business. This is not an earned designation.

Registered representatives, also known as stock-brokers or account executives, often refer to themselves as financial advisors. However, registered representatives are essentially securities salespeople who are not required to have completed financial planning training. Most work for brokerage firms licensed by the SEC or various stock exchanges. Registered representatives earn commissions on the purchase and sale of securities. This means that their recommendations may be based on their financial interests, not yours. Buyer beware.

Different levels of registered representative exist. Those who pass the Series 7 Exam are allowed to sell general securities such as stocks, bonds, mutual funds, and variable annuities. Those who pass the Series 6 Exam are limited to selling mutual funds and variable annuities. Both must also be registered with a member of the Financial Industry Regulatory Authority or a self-regulatory organization and be licensed in each state in which they conduct business.

Registered Investment Advisors (RIA)

RIAs are also individuals or firms that receive compensation for providing advice on securities. RIAs receive their designation by registering with the SEC and/or state securities agencies as investment advisors. Most RIAs charge management fees based on a percentage of the amount of assets they manage. In some instances, RIAs will also be registered representatives who sell investments and charge a commission.

TYPES OF INSURANCE AGENTS

Insurance Agents

Insurance agents are not financial advisors. Some agents only sell insurance products for one company; independent agents or insurance brokers sell insurance products issued by more than one company. Insurance Agents must be licensed by states where they sell life, health, property, and/or casualty insurance, and fixed and variable annuities.

Charted Life Underwriter (CLU)

In the insurance industry, a CLU is the most respected designation. Candidates must take 5 courses in life insurance and financial planning that concentrate heavily on life insurance laws, regulations, and ethics. In addition to their life insurance expertise, CLUs tend to be well educated in estate planning techniques. To maintain the designation, a CLU must complete 30 hours of continuing education each year.

SENIOR ADVISORS AND CONSULTANTS

Certified Senior Advisor® (CSA)

The Society of Certified Senior Advisors® confers the CSA designation. While this designation suggests the advisor is well educated in senior financial matters, the curriculum takes a 3-1/2 day class and a passing score on an exam.

As you can see, myriad designations exist in the financial and insurance industry. Each has legal limitations. Problems occur when salespeople provide advice on securities without the appropriate qualifications or licensure.

For example, an insurance salesperson or bank employee trying to sell you an annuity may recommend that you cash out your stocks, bonds, or mutual funds to purchase the annuity. In doing so, the advisor breaks the law and may not even be aware of it. Recommending that you buy the annuity is legal under the Investment Advisors Act because fixed annuities and indexed annuities are considered insurance contracts rather than investments. The recommendation to sell your stocks, bonds, or mutual funds is investment advice, which insurance salespeople and bank employees may not legally provide.

Protect yourself from conflicts of interest and unqualified advice by making sure you pay for advice, not for commissions on products. Don't be fooled by designations you don't understand and don't take financial advice from insurance salespeople. Even more important, don't take financial advice from your neighbor over the back fence. If you've made the mistake before, you don't have to make it again.

CHAPTER 22

CONSOLIDATE ASSETS

SMART INVESTORS RESPECT THE WISDOM of developing a well-diversified investment portfolio and spreading their risks. Many smart investors still make mistakes when trying to develop such a portfolio. For example, it's easy to think you've accomplished diversification by accumulating various investments spread across a number of different firms. It's also easy to build a portfolio involving multiple firms inadvertently.

Here are some possible scenarios that might lead to a portfolio involving multiple firms.

- You bought a proprietary product that could not be transferred after you purchased it.
- You have a 401k from a former employer.
- You have a Dividend Reinvestment Program Account held directly with the transfer agent.
- You have assets from a long deceased relative.
- You set up a brokerage account with an old friend who is no longer in the picture.

- You or your spouse inherited securities from your parents, and it seemed easiest to keep those securities at their original place.
- You have CDs at several different banks.

Accounts can accumulate over time for many reasons. Over time, however, you may no longer be sure of what you have, where you have it, or how it is performing. It can be an impossible task to stay on top of things, especially as you grow older. It a big mistake to try.

Obviously, your financial affairs will have a different look, feel, and strategy during your accumulation phase of life versus your distribution phase. During the accumulation years, there is a lower sense of urgency to consolidate. You have time to make up for shortcomings. During the distribution years, the story is different because it may be too late to recover from mistakes.

Consolidating your accounts and investments can provide you with ease and convenience, along with tangible and financially quantifiable benefits. Many high net worth folks agree it's best to merge, purge, and work with only one adviser in a quest to streamline. Consolidating allows you to do the following.

1. Intelligently Structure Your Asset Allocation
   The most important component of your investment performance is asset allocation. If you don't know your asset allocation—or it takes big effort to calculate this allocation—it's time to make adjustments. Make sure you are in the mode of

managing investments rather than simply collecting them.

Accumulating too many accounts and too many investments can actually create risk rather than adding diversification. It's like betting on the same horse multiple times—with each individual bet, your risk grows, even though you have many tickets! This is very different from betting on a number of horses or a number of sporting events.

Consolidation allows you to optimize your asset allocation and achieve the most efficient diversification. It allows you to easily recognize when it is time to rebalance.

2. Increase Control and Monitor Goals
   Taking control of your portfolio and making your investments work effectively toward your goals are among the most compelling reasons to consolidate multiple accounts. If you have investments in several locations, it's difficult to stay in control of your overall portfolio. It's also complicated to make your investments work together. In fact, you could be duplicating exposure to certain asset classes. When you consolidate, it's much easier to take charge of your strategy and maintain the intended asset allocation. Moreover, rebalancing is a much simpler task in one account.

   Some investors like to compare the performance of one firm or adviser to another. If you are doing this, be careful you are comparing apples to apples. It is easier to understand how all of your investments are performing when you receive one consolidated report from one provider.

3. Manage Cash Flow
Consolidating may improve the quality of certain planning activities, such as retirement income planning. Typically, you need to determine a sustainable distribution rate (typically 3% to 5%), meet minimum required distributions (4% plus), and monitor your assets to make sure you're not distributing principal and depleting assets more quickly than necessary.

4. Strategically Reduce Your Tax Load
Bringing retirement accounts and brokerage accounts together with a single provider may make it easier for you to implement a tax-efficient investment strategy. For instance, taking advantage of tax-loss harvesting may be easier when your gains and losses are all in the same account.

Work with a qualified professional to ensure that the timing and conditions of your choice to consolidate work to reduce your tax burden. For example, a qualified professional will help you to avoid incurring capital gains tax and surrender charges.

For certain assets, you'll need to figure out whether consolidating will force you to liquidate certain investments and possibly incur tax consequences. For example, investors with company stock in their 401(k) or other workplace retirement plan might lose the option to elect net unrealized appreciation (NUA) if they roll those assets into an IRA.

For annuity investors, it's essential to review the surrender charge policy and possibly adjust the timing of your consolidation to avoid excess expense in the process.

5. Lower Your Costs
   When you invest through multiple providers, you run the risk of paying more fees than necessary—because financial providers typically set asset and trading thresholds before offering price breaks. As a rule, the more assets you move to one financial services provider, the more opportunities you may have to avoid some account fees (such as IRA Custodian Fees) and pay lower fund expenses. Moreover, with most wealth management firms, the more assets under administration, the lower the fee.

6. Receive Better Service
   A relationship with a financial advisor can be very rewarding. In a perfect world, all clients are treated equally. The reality is that the largest clients get better service. By having $100,000 at 10 different institutions, you risk receiving minimal service at each institution. If you consolidate these accounts at one institution, chances are you will get significantly better service.

7. Plan for Your Surviving Spouse or Other Heirs
Perhaps the biggest benefit of consolidating your assets is the one most of us don't want to consider. If you were to pass on, I'm confident you would not want your spouse to be on an asset scavenger hunt. You would not want your life partner or other heirs to need to dig through documents and old statements trying to find the assets. Consolidation can make a big difference to your heirs during this emotionally devastating time.

With your accounts spread out across different firms and different banks, a surviving spouse or heirs could spend months trying to figure things out. Even worse, your loved one might never find orphaned positions and accounts.

Consolidation also helps you make smart decisions about your estate. You can track what you own, how the accounts are titled, and who will be getting what. Consolidation also reduces the chance of forgetting to update the beneficiaries on your accounts.

8. Simplify Your Life
Consolidation means you have fewer firms to deal with. This means you spend less time servicing your affairs and more time managing them. You have fewer meetings, less paperwork, and less clutter. This equals less time required to do any task. If you have to see two or three advisers every time you need to make a modification to your investment plan, you waste your own precious time.

Consolidation also allows you to see the big picture and have online access to your entire portfolio. With accounts at different institutions, you
need to get online access for each. What's more, it
is unlikely that you will be able to transfer funds
electronically between institutions. Consolidation
can make such transfers much easier.

Clearly, there are so many benefits to consolidating your
assets. If you've been making the mistake of spreading your
investments across multiple firms, it's time to correct this
mistake.

CHAPTER 23

WATCH OUT FOR THE TWIN DEVILS: SHAME AND GUILT

F ROM A FINANCIAL PERSPECTIVE, there are two kinds of people in the world: savers and spenders. As a CFP®, I don't see the spenders. If you have money, you see them, perhaps more often than you'd like. Spenders have the instinct to seek out savers the way bees have the instinct to seek out nectar. What's more, while spenders don't have the ability to hold onto money, they are experts at using shame and guilt to acquire it.

If you want your money to last through your retirement years, you must sharpen your skills in resisting shame and guilt. Here are some of the common ways these twin devils can get you.

GUILT OVER PARENTING MISTAKES AND/OR DIVORCE

If you are a parent, you've made mistakes, and some of those mistakes were likely big ones. Parents who feel they are failing (or feel they have already failed) their kids naturally want to make up for it. In cases of divorce or excessive commitments at work, guilt can lead to an unconscious strategy of making up for imperfect parenting by buying expensive toys. In other words, guilt can cause us to try to buy affection we think we do not otherwise deserve.

This strategy can get out of hand quickly. Kids sense guilt and take advantage of it. They take on an entitlement mentality. Before long, parents find themselves buying expensive cars and houses for grown kids and wonder how they got there. It's a case of the guilt trip, one purchase at a time. Nip this habit in the bud when your kids are young. Adjust your lifestyle to give your kids the gift of your time, even if things in the family aren't perfect.

If your adult kids pressure you to give them money, tell them to wait. They will get their inheritance in due time.

SHAME IN FRONT OF WEALTHY PEERS

People who travel in social circles in which their friends have more money than they do often spend more than they can afford out of fear of embarrassment or fear of losing those friends. The overspending often happens gradually. For example, a couple might begin by joining friends out for dinner more frequently than the couple can afford. This grows to vacations, cars, second homes, etc., that they can't afford.

If you are spending more than you can afford to keep up with friends or relatives, your future is at risk. You will at some point run out of money. Then, you'll not only be embarrassed, you'll be broke and maybe even homeless.

One of my clients had to sell her home at age 80 and move to an apartment because she overspent in response to peer pressure. If you are overspending to "keep up," face the problem now when you can preserve your assets for the future. Don't kid yourself: The average life expectancy is growing all the time.

SHAME IN HAVING MORE MONEY THAN EXTENDED FAMILY MEMBERS

Most of us are taught at a young age to be loyal to our immediate and extended family members. Because of this, we may feel guilty if we have much more than extended family members do, even if we've earned our wealth. On the flip side, extended family members can feel justified in coming to us repeatedly for gifts and loans. After all, family members are supposed to help each other.

For example, a woman whose deceased brother's adult kids came to her repeatedly to ask for loans found herself in this situation. Each time, they promised and then failed to pay back the loan. Something in this woman's concept of family loyalty caused her to keep giving loans and gifts, to the point that she couldn't afford them.

While you might seem well balanced in comparison to this woman, it's still a good idea to examine your giving and loaning to family members and/or close friends. Do you give out of guilt or a sense of shame? Do you give more than you can afford?

SHAME SURROUNDING DYSFUNCTION

Whether we want to admit it or not, we all are touched by dysfunction and/or entitlement in some way. In some families, the problem is an adult child who lives at home and doesn't work. In other families, the problem is addiction. In others, a young adult is always studying but never completes an education. In still others, adult kids expect parents to buy their houses as well as fund expensive schools and toys for the grandkids.

From a distance, it's easy to say we shouldn't enable others. In practice, these situations often involve confusion, shame, and/or long-established patterns. We might feel shame that we've contributed to the dysfunction in some way, if only in failing to set limits long ago. We might be confused about what constitutes enabling and what constitutes loyalty. We might be afraid of what will happen if we pull back our financial support.

If you find yourself chronically overfunding, especially if you can't afford it, seek an objective opinion about your situation. Dysfunction rarely rights itself unless someone sets a limit or makes a significant change. Don't let shame or confusion eat away at your assets.

We all feel urges toward guilt and shame. It's part of the human condition. Giving in to these feelings not only fails to solve problems, it can impoverish us. The best way to combat these urges is to step back and take an objective look at our patterns. If we've made mistakes with our kids, we need to acknowledge them and take healthy steps to overcome them. Sometimes we'll need professional help to accomplish that. If we've been overfunding and/or overindulging, we need to reassess our values and set limits. It takes a lot of courage to set limits, but it's the only way to overcome entitlement and dysfunction.

CONCLUSION

FINAL THOUGHTS

N
EARLY EVERY DAY BRINGS NEWS about a medical discovery that may lead to a cure for cancer, heart disease, or another potential killer. In other words, nearly every day we learn that we have the potential to live longer than we ever dreamed possible. While this is great news, it can also be scary.

With life expectancy in the developed countries making its way toward 90, protecting and growing our money is more critical than ever. The quality of our elderly years will be in large part determined by the amount of money we have available to finance our housing, health care, and entertainment needs. The more we've saved the more choices we will have.

Whatever money you have today is your million, and your million is at risk. As I learned in my brief stint at a firm pushing penny stocks, intentional swindlers are alive and well. But intentional swindlers are only one of many threats to your money. Unintentional swindlers, taxes, inflation, family members, and even your own ego can whittle away at your million. In the pages of this book, you've read about each of these and more in detail. I hope you'll return to this book often as a resource to help you protect and grow your million.

For now, as you close the pages of the book, keep in mind the following points.

- Any charmer claiming you are extra special and therefore entitled to above-market returns is likely an intentional swindler. If a promise seems too good to be true, don't believe the promise.

- Financial and insurance salespeople who earn a commission for selling a product have an inherent conflict of interest. Their income depends on selling the product, whether or not that product is a good fit for you.

- People who have good intentions may be unintentional swindlers, if only because they give unqualified and incomplete advice. When a golf buddy or neighbor offers insider information, avoid acting on the tip. When a salesclerk describes why you need a maintenance plan on an electronic product, politely decline the offer.

- Money is a complex family affair, and it's unrealistic to expect smooth sailing without effort. Talk about the money messages you and your spouse bring to the marriage from childhood. Come to agreement about money values, acceptable levels of risk, and the lessons you want to teach your children. Be intentional about teaching financial responsibility at each step of your children's development.

- Children can be adept at manipulating from the youngest ages. Kids want what they want, and they will pull on your heartstrings to get it. Giving in to your kids doesn't help them grow into responsible adults. If you find yourself buying frequent or expensive gifts, be wary of your own motives. If you are buying to make up for guilt feelings for a divorce or other unfortunate circumstance, make a change—and fast.

- If you have an adult child who fails to take responsibility for his or her own finances, communicate and enforce clear boundaries. Even if you've gotten into the habit of giving in to your adult child's demands, you have to stop it. You might need your savings to support you and your significant other for 20 or 30 years to come.

- The time to clarify your values surrounding retirement is long before your retirement age. "Happy retirement" can have a range of definitions depending on a person's values. Some retirees value a house full of grandchildren while others prefer to live in a golf community surrounded by seniors. Financial health is intricately tied to quality of life, but it's not the only factor.

- Retirement comes with special financial challenges, including the realities of inflation and the possible need to finance long-term health care. To face these challenges, consider delaying your Social Security payments for a few years. Investigate long-term health insurance. Be sure you understand your options before making your decision.

- Taxes are complicated and costly. Learn the government rules and regulations so you know the game well enough to win. Take steps to pay the least amount of taxes with your ordinary income, your capital gains, and your estate.

- When emotions are entangled with money, people make bad decisions. Carefully separate your emotions from financial decisions, including those surrounding taxes, kids, and inheritance. The ability to say no is one of the most important ways to protect your money.

- Distinguish between needs and wants. Do not allow yourself to indulge in wants you can't afford. Model this for your children. Keep this discipline even when friends seem to be spending freely. Say no to unnecessary debt.

- A person's ego can be the greatest swindler of all. Pay careful attention to signs that your own ego is a threat to your financial health. For example, if you think you are smarter than everyone else, you are at risk of poor decisions. If you believe you are the best person to handle every aspect of your finances even though you don't have time to research, you are deluded. The need to control everything is a financial liability.

- For the benefit of your family and your future, find the courage to trust the appropriate professional. For your financial affairs, the appropriate professional is a fiduciary, who is both an expert in the financial arena and obligated to keep your best interests as top priority.

- When dealing with financial and insurance professionals, know what the various designations mean. Some are earned, and some come merely by virtue of registering to do business in a certain category. The experience of the provider, the payment structure, and the ethical standards differ widely. A CFP® is the most respected financial advisor designation.

- We all make mistakes involving money, especially with our children and other family members. Don't let the twin devils of shame and guilt torture you. Make peace with your mistakes and move forward.

- Emotionally drained family members don't make the best decisions, especially when asked to do so in a short period surrounding a death. Your careful planning can relieve your family members of extra burdens while protecting the assets you leave.

Protecting your million is one of the most important things you can do to ensure you have a healthy and happy future. If you have money, you will always be a target of a swindler, the government, family members, health care costs, and more. You are even at risk from your own ego. In each of these areas, however, you can take steps to protect your million. Start taking the steps today. Your future is at stake!

ABOUT THE AUTHOR

WARD GARNER

A SENIOR VICE PRESIDENT AND FINANCIAL ADVISOR with Bill Few Associates, Inc., Ward is a CERTIFIED FINANCIAL PLANNER™ (CFP®) who is committed to serving his clients with expertise and integrity. For the last 25+ years, Ward has built strong relationships with clients, helping them achieve their financial goals through clear communication, careful asset allocation, and long-term planning. He advises clients on all aspects of financial planning, including retirement planning, investing, tax planning, estate planning, and elder care planning, as well as charitable giving.

Ward is a Veteran of the U.S. Air Force and an active Rotarian. Ward's service to the community includes the following:

- Member, Advisory Board for Allegheny County Department of Human Services—Office of Children, Youth & Families
- Member, Advisory Board for Allegheny County Department of Human Services—Area Agency on Aging

- District Governor Elect, 2017-2018, Rotary District 7300
- Member, The Paul Harris Society, Paul Elder Chapter of the Rotary Foundation
- Member, The Founders' Society, University of Pittsburgh at Bradford
- Recipient of the U.S. Air Force Achievement Medal (1980-1985)

Ward is a graduate of the University of Pittsburgh with a bachelor's degree in business management.

He lives in Wexford, PA with his wife, Lori. Ward enjoys trap shooting, motorcycling, fly-fishing, and frequent trips to his country home in New Bethlehem, PA.

To contact the author, Ward Garner, visit:

Website ....: HowToProtectMyMillion.com
Email ....: HowToProtectMyMillion@gmail.com
LinkedIn.........: www.linkedin.com/in/wardgarner
Facebook .....: www.facebook.com/HowToProtectMyMillion/

"*I think of my clients as family. Treating clients as family requires empathy and a sense of wanting to protect them, similar to the Rotary promise of "Service Above Self."*

— Ward Garner